Nova Nicaea - Let´s Build Up a Christian-Libertarian Polity!

Jonathan Weinert

Published by Jonathan Weinert, 2024.

While every precaution has been taken in the preparation of this book, the publisher assumes no responsibility for errors or omissions, or for damages resulting from the use of the information contained herein.

NOVA NICAEA - LET´S BUILD UP A CHRISTIAN-LIBERTARIAN POLITY!

First edition. January 8, 2024.

ISBN: 979-8224533367

Written by Jonathan Weinert.

Table of Contents

....1

Preface 2

1 – Introduction 6

2 – Christian Libertarianism is not liberal Christianity 13

3 – Theories of the state and liberal thought leaders...................19

3.1 – Constitutional order in the Mosaic Law 20

3.2 – Constitutional theories of the ancient philosophers and the structure of the republics of Athens and Rome.................................27

3.3 – Thought leader of liberalism and libertarianism 30

3.3.1 – Introduction...31

3.3.2 – John Locke 33

3.3.3 – Charles de Secondat, Baron de Montesquieu 37

3.3.4 – Adam Smith...41

3.3.5 – Silvio Gesell...43

3.3.6 – Milton Friedman..45

3.3.7 – Hans-Adam II. von und zu Liechtenstein 49

3.3.8 – Titus Gebel 50

4 – Sovereignty and international tolerance 55

5 – Constitution of Nova Nicaea...61

5.1 – Central constitutional principles 62

5.2 – The social contract 65

5.3 – Ecumenical community instead of state church 68

5.4 – Duties of citizens 71

5.5 – The Nicaean monarchy 72

5.6 – Implementation of the balance of powers...........................77

5.7 – Federalism...89

6 – Economic and social policies 92

6.1 – Capitalism as a law of nature 93

6.2 – Private property...95

6.2.1 – Acquisition of private property in general.........................96

6.2.2 – Private ownership of land and property.............................97

6.2.3 – Land ownership in Nova Nicaea 102

6.2.4 – The function of money 104

6.2.5 – Currency system in Nova Nicaea...................................... 108

6.3 – Welfare system and public income 116

7 – Education 120

8 – Language policy.. 122

9 – Defense, military and civil protection.................................... 127

10 – Realization of a Christian-libertarian polity 129

10.1 – Sovereignty over a territory 130

10.2 – Gradual design.. 133

10.3 – Colonization of an empty territory 140

Annex 142

A1 – Draft social contract Nova Nicaea...................................... 143

A2 – Nova Nicaea constitutional scheme 146

Jonathan Weinert

Nova Nicaea

-

Let´s Build Up a
Christian-Libertarian Polity!

Preface

„You are the salt of the earth; but if the salt loses its flavor, how shall it be seasoned? It is then good for nothing but to be thrown out and trampled underfoot by men. You are the light of the world. A city that is set on a hill cannot be hidden. Nor do they light a lamp and put it under a basket, but on a lampstand, and it gives light to all who are in the house. Let your light so shine before men, that they may see your good works and glorify your Father in heaven." (Mt. 5,13-16)

I haven't been able to get this Bible quote out of my head for years. For me, this is a mission that our God makes shine up again and again in my thoughts. This saying of Jesus forbids me passivity – a state of waiting that I perceive in many Christians. Jesus was not passive, nor were his disciples. And over the past 2,000 years, millions of faithful Christians have blessed the world, both on a small and large scale.

When Christians come together for worship on Sunday, praise, glory and thanksgiving ascend to God's throne - and certainly also a lot of prayer, supplication and intercession. This is wonderful and important - or as traditional liturgies put it: truly meet and right. But something else, probably even more important, happens during the service: streams of blessing flow down on Christianity through God's word and acts of worship (the old church divisions refer to these as "sacraments" or "mysteries"). Afterwards, the faithful leave the house of God and go out into the world - the world that so urgently needs God's blessing, protection and light! As Christians, we have the task of taking the blessing out into the world and not keeping it to ourselves - because we are the salt of the earth and the light of the world (or at least we should be). This fact is expressed particularly beautifully in a blessing at the end of many Latin mass liturgies, where the congregation is called out: „Ite, missa est!", which can be roughly translated as "Go, this is a mission!".

How can we live up to this claim? By preaching and proselytizing to those around us? Certainly, one or the other has the gift of leading people to Jesus with words. However, if all Christians were to talk at their fellow human beings, the impression of "pious chatterboxes" would quickly arise, with whom no one can do anything. Instead, our life and work must be a channel of blessing for those around us. This begins in the family, continues in professional life and ultimately encompasses all areas of life - including, of course, the public sphere and thus social coexistence. Most Christians live in more or less democratically constituted states in which state power emanates from the people. Every single citizen of a democracy bears a small part of the responsibility for the well-being of society. No one can shirk this responsibility - certainly not a Christian.

For this reason, I too have become politically involved and strive to have a beneficial impact on this world. However, anyone who becomes politically active as a Christian in today's Western countries should bear two things in mind:

- In the history of mankind, every civilization had a certain lifespan and then more or less disappeared from the scene. This often happened due to violent upheavals but was also partly caused by the fact that the civilization in question became dysfunctional and failed, paving the way for foreign powers. There are some indications that this is exactly what Western civilization or parts of it could be facing in the coming decades.

- While in past centuries entire peoples of the Western world were Christian and there was a consensus in society that people lived in a Christian state, this is no longer the case today. You can regret this or simply accept it. God allows everyone free will and does not force anything on anyone - so we should not try to do that either. For this reason, libertarianism as a consistent variety of liberalism seems most appropriate to me as a Christian.

In my view, the following saying from the early church can serve as the guiding principle of Christian liberalism:

In necessariis unitas,
in dubiis libertas,
in omnibus caritas.
In the necessary unity,
liberty in doubt,
charity in all things.

Two years ago, I started writing a book entitled "Faith, State and Liberty", in which I wanted to derive the Christian-libertarian political approach I advocate on the basis of the Bible, world history and the works of important state and social theorists (from antiquity to the present day) and provide food for thought for the political practice of Christians today. Two scenarios were always to be contrasted: the ideal image of a Christian polity and its application in the secular state.

I didn't have the time to finish the book as quickly as I would have liked, mainly due to my job as the manager of a sales team. When the theoretical derivation part was finished and I was in the middle of the second part, I therefore decided to split the book up for the time being and initially focus only on the (still) fictitious Christian polity in the application part and possibly add chapters on application in existing states later.

I was prompted to do so on the one hand by the precipitating global political events following the Russian invasion of Ukraine, and on the other by the emergence of the Free Cities movement in recent years. The first of these aspects highlights the decline of the former Christian nations and the resulting need for alternative social constructs more clearly than before. The second aspect is a ray of hope that leads to the assumption that the establishment of an exemplary

Christian community could possibly be implemented much more easily and quickly than I would have suspected a few months ago.

This is why my book on the possibility of a Christian-libertarian polity is now available.

1 – Introduction

I already mentioned in the foreword that I have two scenarios in mind when considering Christian-based engagement in politics and society:

- The Christian polity: by this I mean a society in which there is a consensus that living together must be based on Christian values
- Political activity by Christians within an existing state in which this consensus does not exist - i.e. currently the norm

As I no longer see much chance of success for the second case, I am focusing on the first scenario in this book.

The example of ancient Israel shows us that a kind of "theocracy" is possible. The Law of Moses directly commanded the people of the Old Covenant to live according to God's will. After the Christianization of the European peoples, their laws and state regulations were also derived in part from biblical teachings. As long as everyone agrees that the Bible and Christian teachings are the standard for living together, this works. Today, deriving political decisions from the Christian faith is hardly discussed any more. And that is quite understandable, as Christian values and Christian faith have been increasingly relegated to the private sphere in recent decades. We no longer live in a Christian state and should not pretend that we do. In today's multi-religious society, it would simply be presumptuous of us Christians to want to impose rules on our fellow human beings that are derived from our faith. It is therefore neither possible nor appropriate to make political decisions in a multi-religious society in the same way as they could be made in a purely Christian state.

I believe it is possible and desirable to build a Christian polity even in this day and age. If a sufficient number of volunteers can be found to get such a project off the ground, I will give it my all. However, it must never be an attempt to impose our convictions on those who think or believe differently. Rather, I envision building a Christian civilization from scratch in an uninhabited area - as a beacon from which the light of the world can shine far and wide. A city on a mountain in biblical parlance.

Does that sound utopian? Perhaps. But is it impossible? Certainly not! We have several precedents in our time where something comparable has been achieved. Firstly, the modern state of Israel, which was established as the home of the Jews and has established itself and is functioning despite much resistance and hostility. I will come back to this later. The second predominantly positive example that comes to mind are the United Arab Emirates and Dubai in particular. Anyone who visited this area a hundred years ago would have come across a few desert villages. Today, there is an ultra-modern urban society there that is ahead of Western societies in many respects, but above all is significantly more developed than the surrounding area. To a certain extent, this also applies to the city-state of Singapore, which (having emerged from a small British trading post) has become an economic and social center of great appeal in the Asian region. Now I am far from describing Singapore, Dubai or Israel as ideal states (otherwise I could emigrate there) - but we can learn from the willpower and pioneering spirit of the people responsible for building these states. I am amazed at how the sheikhs of Dubai have managed to build a highly developed society within a few decades on the basis of Islam and liberalism (which many of their fellow believers regard as irreconcilable opposites) - on the other hand, I feel great regret and a certain shame that nothing similar has been produced from the bosom of Christendom for a long time.

Recently, the Free Cities movement has been spreading among libertarians (the term used today to describe supporters of classical liberalism - in contrast to today's so-called liberals, who usually have little more in common with the original liberalism than the name).

The basic idea of this movement is to buy uninhabited areas and, with the consent of the respective state, to build free private cities there, i.e. partially sovereign alternative social structures on a small scale. Within this concept, I also see an excellent opportunity to establish small Christian communities or polities.

In some respects, I see the emergence of the state of Israel as a model for a possible Christian polity, even if I cannot quite understand the unconditional support of some Christians for the policies of a Jewish state. There have probably been Jews at all times since the destruction of Jerusalem by the Romans who have longed for the land of their fathers. However, the idea only became concrete at the end of the 19th century when Theodor Herzl put this desire on paper under the impression of the anti-Semitism that was spreading in Europe at the time. He wrote the book "Der Judenstaat" / "The Jewish State" and presented his fellow believers with the idea of establishing a modern Jewish state. Just half a century later, the state of Israel was a reality.

With regard to his visionary idea, Theodor Herzl is a role model for me. Even if the situation of the Jews at that time was different from the situation of us Christians today - there are parallels. Just like the Jews back then, believing Christians are a minority in Western countries today. To a certain extent, this means that Christians are socially marginalized and withdraw from the public eye. The situation of our brothers and sisters in faith in other parts of the world, where they are marginalized, openly persecuted and sometimes threatened with death, is even more similar to the situation of the Jews in Europe at the end of the 19th and beginning of the 20th century. Due to the current minority status of committed Christians, the church and Christianity are (unfortunately justifiably) losing more and more of their social influence and are becoming increasingly insignificant as shaping factors.

Nevertheless, Christianity has the task of shining a light into the world and contributing to the well-being of nations. Since Christian teaching and Christian life cannot fully unfold their effect in a secular society, it makes sense to build a Christian polity from scratch, as a kind of social experiment and to show the world what is possible with a Christian attitude to life.

I can hardly imagine that there are fewer believing Christians in the world today than there were Jews a hundred years ago. For this reason alone, the realization of a Christian polity should be possible with ease. The conditions for its realization are also better than the conditions were for the founding of the state of Israel. The project can theoretically be tackled anywhere in the world because we Christians do not have a common historical homeland. All that is needed is a previously uninhabited patch of earth and a government that is prepared to make this territory available to us (in the form of a purchase or lease agreement).

In addition to the parallels between Herzl's Zionist concerns and my idea of founding a Christian polity, there are also clear differences. The most serious lies in the different character of the two biblical religions. While Judaism defines itself not only as a religious community but also as a nation, Christianity has an international mission. It is to bring God's word and salvation to all peoples. Unlike Judaism, Christianity cannot and must not withdraw into a single state. It is therefore inconceivable to bring all Christians together in one state. Since even the complete emigration of the Jews to Israel has not happened, the complete relocation of all Christians to a newly founded polity is neither to be expected nor desired.

A Christian polity would be less of a "homeland" and more of a model and pattern, perhaps a crystallization point for exchange with one another and ecumenism, if necessary, an escape point for individuals. In this respect, it would be comparable to city states of other cultures, such as Singapore or Dubai, which exist as beacons of civilization in interaction with the surrounding cultural circles and represent engines of progress.

It is also possible that the founding of a Christian polity will lead to other world views (not necessarily religions, but political schools of thought, for example) following suit and establishing their own model states, thereby defusing conflicts in the internal politics of existing states. I am convinced that any social idea has a greater chance of success if it is not imposed on those affected, but if those involved are volunteers without exception. As a convinced economic liberal, I am absolutely not a friend of socialism. However, I would not rule out the possibility that it can work if all those involved are determined to make it a success, i.e., if a socialist social order is built up from volunteers who also feel comfortable in the system they have established. Only if such an effect can have a positive influence on social peace within existing states is the foundation of the Christian polity worthwhile.

On the subject of feasibility, I would like to quote Theodor Herzl at this point, which in my opinion can also be applied to today:

"In presenting the idea, I have to contend with a danger. If I say all the things that lie in the future with restraint, it will seem as if I don't believe in their possibility myself. If, on the other hand, I announce the realization without reservation, everything will easily look like a fantasy. That is why I say clearly and firmly: I believe in the possibility of its realization, even if I do not presume to have found the final form of the idea. The Jewish state is a world need, therefore it will come into being. It would be a rather crazy story if pursued by any one individual - but if many Jews go in for it at the same time, it is perfectly reasonable, and its realization offers no difficulties worth mentioning. The idea depends only on the number of its followers."[1]

It is the same with a Christian polity - as an individual I will not be able to establish it. But if a sufficient number of brothers and sisters in faith join the idea (either as emigrants or as supporters or investors), it will succeed with God's help.

In all these considerations, everyone should be aware that a Christian polity, indeed even a Christian state, can never be a kingdom of heaven on earth, nor can it provide for the eternal life of its citizens. Rather, its officials should be aware that there is something higher, the development of which should be hindered as little as possible by the government. Likewise, experience teaches us that the Christian faith is lived in very different forms and facets that exist side by side. Although it should be the ambition of a Christian government to strengthen the bond of unity and peace within Christianity and it should be the heartfelt wish of all Christians that the unity of the Church should once again become visible (for there can only be one Church because it is the bride of Christ and Christ does not practise polygamy), it is not for any Christian or any Christian government to rise above the brethren and interfere with the freedom of conscience in matters of detail. How I envision this balancing act will become clear at some points in the book.

To emphasize that I am serious about its realization, I would like to give the Christian polity a name at this point, which I will also use in the following chapters. Because I consider the realization in the form of a city-state or a free private city to be more realistic than the establishment of a larger territorial state, it should have a reference to the ancient city-states. As the unity of the whole church is very important to me, this aspect should also be reflected in the name. That's why I came across the city of Nicaea in Asia Minor, where one of the great councils of early Christianity took place, which adopted the original "Nicene Creed", which is still the most widely recognized in Christendom today.

For this reason, I am giving the social project initiated here the name "**Nicaea**" (or "**Nova Nicaea**" where it seems necessary to differentiate) and also using the word "**Nicaean**" as an adjective. A small note on this name: ancient Nicaea is known to have been in Asia Minor and therefore in the Greek-speaking area. The correct pronunciation of the name is therefore not "Nicea", as is often used today, but "Nikaia" (even in the original Latin pronunciation, the C was generally pronounced as K and the sequence of letters AE as AI).

The Creed adopted in Nicaea is still used today (mostly in the expanded form of the Nicene-Constantinopolitan Creed) in the services of countless church congregations. Its original form reads:

I believe in one God, the Father Almighty, the Creator of everything visible and invisible.

And in the one Lord Jesus Christ, the Son of God, who is begotten as the only begotten of the Father, that is, from the essence of the Father, God from God, light from light, true God from true God, begotten, not created, of a being with the father (homoousion to patri); through whom all things in heaven and on earth came into being; who for us men and because of our salvation descended and became flesh, became human, suffered and rose again on the third day, ascended to heaven, will come to judge the living and the dead;

And in the Holy Spirit.

Due to the cross-confessional agreement to this confession, I advocate defining it in the constitution of Nicaea as the foundation of society and making agreement to it a condition for citizenship alongside valid baptism in the name of the triune God. Every polity needs a common constituent element. In the case of nation states, this is typically membership of a nation, a people. In a Christian community, this element can be nothing other than the combination of faith and baptism.

2 – Christian Libertarianism is not liberal Christianity

At this point, I would like to take the precaution of avoiding a misunderstanding, as it is quite obvious from the way I have expressed it. When I talk about Christian libertarianism, I am by no means referring to liberal Christianity per se. Anyone who knows me knows that I come from a very conservative family and congregation and, if you want to put it that way, am generally a very conservative Christian personally (although I don't particularly like the term "conservative" because everyone understands it differently). To go into how I live the Christian faith and how I personally stand on individual questions of the Christian faith and church doctrine is, in my opinion, inappropriate and too broad in the context of this book. However, I do not rule out the possibility of writing about this in the future, should this book find interest and distribution, as I can imagine that some readers may be interested in.

At this point just this much: I am convinced that God's will is written down in the Bible and that the Bible must therefore be the authoritative norm for life and teaching both for the church and for every individual Christian. In other words, I do not believe that lifestyles or opinions that contradict the Bible are pleasing to God. I am extremely skeptical of modern biblical criticism. Just as we only know which books belong to the Bible from church tradition, I consider church tradition to be the most important tool for interpreting the Bible and I am also a great friend of traditional church liturgy. However, it is important to me that only that which does not contradict Scripture or the unity of the church as a whole is considered tradition.

By liberal Christianity, I mean currents within Christianity that abandon or water down fundamental biblical teachings (such as Jesus' sonship with God, his birth from the Virgin Mary, our redemption from sin through his death, his resurrection from the dead or the hope of Jesus' return in glory as judge of the world), deny the credibility of the Bible as such and thus abandon Christian life to arbitrariness. That is the opposite of what I am striving for.

When I speak and write of Christian libertarianism, I mean the consistent recognition of the fact that God has endowed every single human being with a free will on which even he, the Almighty, imposes nothing. For me, this results in the personal responsibility of each individual as a central component of Christian life and the need to respect this and to interfere as little as possible with freedom of conscience.

If the Lord God does not do violence to the conscience and free will of the individual, no human being should do so - not even a government. This results in the need for mutual tolerance among Christians, but also an acceptance of the fact that not everyone accepts the Christian faith.

In terms of the polity, this means that a government that acts according to Christian standards must therefore grant every individual and every community every freedom that does not interfere with the freedom and rights of other individuals and communities. In this understanding, the polity has the task of ensuring that no one encroaches on the rights of others and that voluntarily agreed contracts are observed. It can prohibit abusive behavior but may not force its citizens to behave in a way that is contrary to their conscience. If individual citizens (for whatever reason) wish to have their lives more strictly regulated, they are free to join with like-minded people to form communities that voluntarily restrict the freedom of the individual more than the surrounding social order. The decisive factor here is free consent to the agreed rules and the possibility of leaving such a community again. Strictly speaking, even the acceptance of citizenship is the entry into such a voluntary association of people (except that the voluntary nature of this is unfortunately very limited in most cases so far).

In the area of personal faith life, Christian libertarianism for me means, firstly, accepting that not all people share my Christian faith and, secondly, tolerating the fact that my fellow believers also live out the common faith differently to some extent than I do and also have a different understanding of this faith in some respects. I deliberately use the different words accept and tolerate here, as the meanings differ in nuances. With the word "acceptance" it is quite clear that it is about taking note of something and respecting it without approving of it (I cannot approve of my fellow human beings rejecting the Christian faith because I am convinced that they will miss out on eternal glory as a result - but I have to respect their personal decision). The term "tolerance" is more elastic - in my understanding it has more to do with goodwill and sympathy. Acceptance is included and in some ways the terms can be used interchangeably, but tolerance goes a little further. Nowadays it is often used to mean a form of approval or agreement. I wouldn't go quite that far, as it is still about opinions or behaviors of my fellow human beings that I don't share. But as a Christian, I have to understand that my personal interpretation is only piecemeal and that there are other views that are not necessarily wrong but can complement and correct me. And even if I completely disagree with a view held by my brother or sister, it is still only up to God to decide who is right. In such a case, my task is to support my fellow Christians in love. That is my understanding of tolerance. To give you an example: My parents brought me to baptism as an infant and I am very grateful to them for making me a child of God and a member of the universal church from the very beginning. My children were also baptized shortly after birth and if you ask me, I will speak out in favour of baptizing young children for various good reasons. However, I am aware that not all members of the faith agree with me on this point and can justify their views. I have to tolerate that - and expect the other side to be tolerant of my point of view.

What does this mean for our behavior in the Christian polity? In Nova Nicaea, all domestic political decisions are based on the common foundation of the Christian faith. If there is a need for the legal regulation of a matter, one can look to the Bible and find a regulation that reflects the meaning of Holy Scripture as well as possible. In civil law, some passages from the Mosaic Law can be adopted one-to-one - for example, the degree of kinship above which marriage is prohibited. At other points, where the Bible is less clear or the continuation of an Old Testament regulation is not compatible with the context of the New Testament, the legislator must transfer as much responsibility as possible to the individual or the church communities. To stay with the example of marriage: Are (certain) church ministers allowed to marry or not? Are there cases in which the remarriage of divorced persons is permissible or does a canonical annulment of marriage (as exists in the Roman Catholic Church) open up the possibility of remarriage? There are different answers and approaches to these and other questions within Christianity. Tolerance must be practiced here and the state must ensure that every citizen has the opportunity to live according to their conscience. The fact that the issues mentioned are serious and controversial is intentional on my part - to show that tolerance within Christianity can also be painful at times (we cannot avoid this as long as Christ does not personally and visibly take over the reigns). Acceptance of orders that clearly contradict Christianity can only exists at the borders of Nicene society. However, under certain circumstances it may also be necessary to apply different standards to foreign visitors than to Christian fellow citizens. However, this should be the exception rather than the rule.

In a secular state, we not only have to practice tolerance among ourselves, but also acceptance towards non-Christians and their lifestyles. This can be even more painful in many cases. I remember the discussions surrounding the introduction of "marriage for all" and can imagine that in the foreseeable future, Western countries will be faced with similar discussions regarding plural marriage. From a biblical perspective, marriage is an institution between a man and a woman, at least according to the New Testament between one man and one woman. In a Christian polity, this can easily be regulated by law and the only question would be how the state deals with citizens who live in other forms of relationships outside the regulated marriage laws. In a state that is not (or no longer) Christian, different lifestyles must be taken into account. In this respect, "marriage for all" was a logical consequence of social reality and, in the same way, opening marriage to more than two people could be the logical consequence again in a few years' time. As Christians, we don't have to like that (and if there had been a referendum on "marriage for all", I would have voted against it). In my view, however, it is not possible to reverse such a development, nor does it make sense for the sake of social peace in a secular society. As Christians, we are called upon here to defend our own freedom of conscience without restricting that of our fellow human beings. A state can instruct its registry offices to marry same-sex couples or even more than two people. Civil registrars who are faithful to the Bible quickly come into conflict of conscience (though sometimes also when remarrying divorced people). If it is not possible for them to see the civil marriage ceremony simply as an administrative act (that would be my personal approach), they should change their profession. What the state is not allowed to do under any circumstances, and what all Christian communities should firmly oppose, is to force a religious community to perform a church wedding in such cases. I have chosen this topic as a current and hotly debated example to show that we should not expect Christian values and morals to be enforced in a non-Christian state. In this sense, Christians should insist that the state interferes as little as possible in private and religious matters, respects the freedom of conscience of the individual and strengthens the autonomy of religious communities.

That is why I consider consistent libertarianism to be the political attitude best suited to biblically faithful Christianity in our time. And it is precisely against the background of these considerations that I see a need for a Christian-libertarian polity.

3 – Theories of the state and liberal thought leaders

3.1 – Constitutional order in the Mosaic Law

Since the earliest times, people have lived together in orderly states. All these states had some form of constitution, sometimes codified in writing, but sometimes only handed down in customs and traditions. One of the earliest written records of such a social order is the Law of Moses. Although its details are not binding for us Christians, it deserves our special attention because it is our firm belief that this law was given to the people of Israel directly by God. Therefore, I would like to begin this chapter on theories of government by exploring what the Old Testament tells us about governmental order.

After the Israelites had left Egypt, experienced their first miracles (provision of water and manna) and defeated the Amalekites with God's help, they were visited by Jetro, Moses' father-in-law. He observed how Moses was busy from morning till night dispensing justice and getting involved in all the small matters of the Israelites. Jetro saw that this situation was not sustainable in the long term and gave Moses the following advice:

„You must be the people's representative before God and bring their disputes to him. Teach them his decrees and instructions, and show them the way they are to live and how they are to behave.

But select capable men from all the people—men who fear God, trustworthy men who hate dishonest gain—and appoint them as officials over thousands, hundreds, fifties and tens. Have them serve as judges for the people at all times, but have them bring every difficult case to you; the simple cases they can decide themselves. That will make your load lighter, because they will share it with you." (Exodus 18, 19b-22)

Moses gratefully accepted the advice and in the subsequent narrative of the wilderness wanderings, these officials appear again and again as the basic structure of Israelite society. They therefore seem to have proved their worth.

We can learn three principles from this:

1. Every state order must see itself as God's instrument for the benefit of the people.
2. Power and responsibility should be decentralized as far as possible. On the one hand (as Jetro explains), this avoids overburdening public officials, and on the other hand, the experience of past millennia shows that too much power accumulated by individuals easily leads to abuse, whereas federalism counteracts this.
3. All office-holders should be selected according to their abilities and trustworthiness.

At this point, I will not go into the details of the Mosaic Law, which can be dealt with appropriately elsewhere (which is why I will also skip the Ten Commandments now, even though I consider them to be essential for human coexistence). For now, I will only deal with what can be applied as basic principles for the functioning of a community. The next noteworthy passage in this context can be found in the 23rd chapter of the second book of Moses:

„Do not follow the crowd in doing wrong. When you give testimony in a lawsuit, do not pervert justice by siding with the crowd, and do not show favoritism to a poor person in a lawsuit." (Exodus 23,2+3)

These verses are remarkable in that they represent (at least as far as I know) the first formulation of the principle of the rule of law. And they also immediately cite two aspects that are likely to undermine this principle: giving in to the masses (which we encounter thousands of years later in Pontius Pilate's method as an outrageous evil) and false consideration for the supposedly or actually weaker. Especially in our day and age, when democracy and consideration for the weaker are rightly held in high esteem, this Bible passage can remind us that these principles, which are good in themselves, have their limits where they restrict legal certainty. An injustice does not become better if it is done for the benefit of the weak or is approved by majority vote. In short: the rule of law is a higher-ranking principle than democracy and the welfare state.

The majority of the remaining chapters of the second, third and fourth books of Moses deal with regulations for worship and civil law. Only a few verses in the 17th chapter of the fifth book of Moses are of importance in terms of state theory. In verses 8-13, the theocratic character of the old Israelite social order comes to the fore in that the priests are appointed as the holders of supreme jurisdiction.

The following verses concern Israelite kingship. I stumbled across this passage once before in my early youth. In my environment, it was widely believed that it was fundamentally wrong of the Israelites to demand that Samuel appoint a king centuries after the conquest of the holy land. That is why, as a young person, I was surprised to find a passage in the Mosaic Law that regulates precisely this appointment of the king. The monarchy seems to be intended and desired by God in principle, but with very clear rules:

„When you enter the land the LORD your God is giving you and have taken possession of it and settled in it, and you say, "Let us set a king over us like all the nations around us," be sure to appoint over you a king the LORD your God chooses. He must be from among your fellow Israelites. Do not place a foreigner over you, one who is not an Israelite."

(Deuteronomy 17, 14+15)

Two principles are recognizable here that are no longer at all modern today, but which the people of Israel should value:

1. The divine right of kingship. Kingship should always derive from God. It is therefore not surprising that the Israelite kings

were installed by priests or prophets through anointing and that this tradition has been preserved in Christian monarchies right up to the present day (Queen Elizabeth and King Charles were also installed as monarch in the coronation ceremony by clergymen of the Church of England through anointing - this part of the ceremony was considered so sacred that it is the only moment of the service that was not filmed and broadcast on television).

2. It was to be one of the brethren, i.e., first among equals. In principle, all foreigners were excluded from the field of candidates, which may seem strange to us today, but was completely logical in the situation of the Israelite people due to their pagan neighbors. Incidentally, several modern constitutions also uphold the principle that no foreigner can become head of state - for example, only those born in the United States can run for the office of US president.

Verses 16 and 17 prohibit the Israelite kings from excessive pomp and an unusually large number of wives (two bad habits that were often associated with monarchies at that time and in later times). From verse 18 onwards, things become highly interesting again in terms of constitutional history:

„When he takes the throne of his kingdom, he is to write for himself on a scroll a copy of this law, taken from that of the Levitical priests. It is to be with him, and he is to read it all the days of his life so that he may learn to revere the LORD his God and follow carefully all the words of this law and these decrees and not consider himself better than his fellow Israelites and turn from the law to the right or to the left. Then he and his descendants will reign a long time over his kingdom in Israel. " (Deuteronomy 17, 18-20)

These verses mean nothing other than that a monarchy that is pleasing to God cannot be an absolute monarchy but must always be a constitutional monarchy. The monarch is bound by law and justice. The protection of these is his foremost task. The last sentence can sometimes be interpreted to mean that the king, once chosen by God, can establish a hereditary monarchy, i.e., pass on the office to his descendants. In my view, however, this conclusion is not compelling.

I find it interesting that the jurisdiction of the priests appears in close proximity to the regulations on kingship. Even if such a theocratic form of jurisdiction is inconceivable in today's states (and I also don't believe that it would be God's will to recreate the state structure of ancient Israel one-to-one today), we are shown a principle here that we are familiar with from modern states: the separation of powers - in this case at least between the judiciary (priests) and the executive (king).

Another instruction that Moses gave to the Israelites and especially to his successor Joshua towards the end of his life seems important to me:

„And Moses commanded them, saying: At the end of every seven years, at the appointed time in the year of release, at the Feast of Tabernacles, when all Israel comes to appear before the Lord your God in the place which He chooses, you shall read this law before all Israel in their hearing.

Gather the people together, men and women and little ones, and the stranger who is within your gates, that they may hear and that they may learn to fear the Lord your God and carefully observe all the words of this law, and that their children, who have not known it, may hear and learn to fear the Lord your God as long as you live in the land which you cross the Jordan to possess." (5.Mose 31, 10-13)

The principle of legal certainty comes up again here. All citizens, including children and foreign nationals, should be regularly informed about the legal regulations and be always aware of the law. The sentence "ignorance is no defense against punishment" is only justified if it is guaranteed that ignorance cannot occur through no fault of one's own. After all, judging or sentencing someone according to a law that they cannot know is a great injustice. This form of legal certainty would also be good for today's societies. However, two widespread evils stand in the way of this: The exuberant abundance of regulations and the constant changes. The fact that law is one of the courses with the highest drop-out rates at many universities, meaning that even students who study the subject full-time fail due to its complexity, should give us a lot to think about. Legal certainty also has something to do with self-restraint on the part of the state and legal continuity.

With this, I conclude this constitutional tour of the Mosaic Law, noting the following principles found therein:

- Responsibility of the government towards God
- Federalism
- Selection of public officials according to ability and trustworthiness
- Rule of law and legal certainty
- Monarchy and divine right
- Constitutionalism
- Principle of "first among equals"
- Separation of powers
- Information of the population

Almost as interesting as what we learn is the fact that some key points of today's constitutions are not mentioned at all. For one thing, how exactly the officials were chosen, and which government officials still supported the king. Secondly (and this is what I find most remarkable), the legislature is apparently completely absent. This may have something to do with the fact that the Mosaic Law itself was considered immutable. As I mentioned above, I also consider legal continuity to be enormously important. However, there are always questions of detail that arise, for example, due to civilizational innovations and require regulation. Decisions on the levying of taxes and labor services or on the state budget (which certainly wasn't called that back then and was also less bloated than it is today) also had to be made by someone. We do not know from the Mosaic Law whether the king was responsible for this, the priests or the assembly of princes over the fathers' houses. At the time of Solomon's son Rehoboam, the issue of labor services in Israel became a political issue that caused the state to collapse. It is therefore not insignificant to look for solutions to such constitutional issues. In the following sections, we will look at constitutions and constitutional theories from antiquity to modern times.

3.2 – Constitutional theories of the ancient philosophers and the structure of the republics of Athens and Rome

A number of treatises on state theory have come down to us from ancient Greece. One of the oldest is Plato's "Politeia", a work on the state written in the form of a conversation. It says about the ideal state:

"that kings must be those who have shown themselves to be the best in philosophy and war."[2]

This idea corresponds very well to the principle in Exodus 18 that office holders should be chosen according to ability and trustworthiness. Such a government is nothing other than an aristocracy or meritocracy.

According to Plato, aristocracy results in worse constitutional forms. First, through the misappointment of state offices, prestige would become more important than ability (timocracy), before state power concentrated on the rich and the poorer were excluded from it (oligarchy). In oligarchy, wealth would become more and more concentrated, creating an ever-growing mass of impoverished people who would eventually revolt and establish a constitution of equality (democracy). As democracy would take on ever more anarchic traits, the call for a strong man would eventually arise and lead to autocracy and tyranny (tyranny).[3]

Like Plato, the philosophers Aristotle and Polybius also saw a succession of constitutions emerging from one another. Both were of the opinion that good and bad forms of government naturally alternated in a perpetual cycle. A monarchy serving the common good would give rise to a tyranny, which would be replaced by an aristocracy, which would then degenerate into an oligarchy. This is followed by an initially good democracy (called politia by Aristotle), which develops into a rule of the poor or the mob (called democracy by Aristotle, ochlocracy by Polybius). From this, or from the resulting chaos, monarchy would again emerge as the rule of a single individual. Both authors therefore advocate a mixed constitution, such as that which existed in the Roman Republic.[4]

I will discuss the structure of the Roman Republic a little later. However, the Greek city-states, in which the ancient philosophers were able to observe the various constitutional forms, emerged much earlier. The best-known example is the polis of Athens, whose constitutional history I will look at below.

According to tradition, Athens was founded thousands of years ago by King Kekrops I. King Theseus established the actual polis, i.e. the city-state. After phases of monarchy, tyranny and aristocracy or oligarchy, Attic democracy emerged.[5]

The transition from aristocracy to democracy took place in the 6th century BC through the reforms of Solon and Cleisthenes. In 594 BC, Solon introduced the participation of broad sections of the population, especially the peasantry, in political power. To this end, the population was divided into four wealth classes, which together formed the People's Assembly as the center of all important decisions. The class distinctions were abolished by Cleisthenes in 508 and 507 BC. Athens was divided into the three regions of city, countryside and coast, each of which was subdivided into 10 trittyes. Three trittyes (one from each region) formed a phyle as a political unit with a representative cross-section of the entire population. The people continued to form the central assembly, but now without class distinctions. Most offices were filled by drawing lots. In the fifth century, Pericles introduced so-called diets as compensation for taking on public office and participating in assemblies. The central principle was the constant change of office holders, so that power could not be consolidated in one hand. Women, slaves and immigrants were excluded from political participation. A major weakness was that the majority decision was almost absolute, which excluded minority rights and led to the abolition of democracy and the introduction of tyranny at the end of the fifth century BC.[6]

The example of the polis of Athens is therefore actually very close to the constitutional cycles of the philosophers. Their call for a mixed form is therefore entirely justified. I will therefore now leave ancient Greece and turn to the Roman constitution at the time of the Republic.

Three different popular assemblies formed the basis of the state structure in the Roman Republic: the comitia centuriata, the comitia tributa and the concilium plebis. The voting rights of the first two bodies were weighted according to property. They elected most of the magistrates, i.e., offices of state, from among whom the members of the senate were appointed. Both the senate and the magistrates could submit legislative proposals, which were voted on in the popular assemblies. The concilium plebis served as a representative of the common people and mainly elected the ten tribunes of the people, who represented a controlling authority of the senate and the magistrates through a right of veto.[7]

As is easy to see, the Roman constitution was a hybrid of aristocracy and democracy. The concilium plebis ensured the participation of all the people and the control of the government by their representatives as far as possible, while the other two assemblies, elected according to tax revenue, were intended to prevent the state from slipping into an "ochlocracy", i.e., the political dominance of the lower classes.

Overall, the Roman Republic was therefore somewhat more stable than the polis of Athens. However, as we all know, it also fell into an existential crisis, which led to the Roman Empire and thus to tyranny.

3.3 – Thought leader of liberalism and libertarianism

3.3.1 – Introduction

The ancient republics had fallen at the time of the birth of Christ and had given way to the Roman Empire of Augustus. This empire still contained some elements of the Roman Republic, but was nothing more than a tyranny. It was this very efficient but not very humane form of government that the emerging church was confronted with. And this form of government was not abolished by Emperor Constantine's adoption of the Christian faith, but at best mitigated. It is therefore not surprising that the early Christian states that emerged from the crumbling empire generally followed this model and were structured as monarchies.

However, the Christian states of the Middle Ages did not yet see themselves as absolute rulerships of individuals, but rather allowed the different classes of society certain rights of co-determination, just as there was no absolute rule in the church at that time. The church in antiquity had a constitution based on the division of tasks, consisting of bishops, priests and deacons. During the period of Christianization, this division of tasks was transferred to the emerging Christian monarchies with varying degrees of intensity, so that the princes had to share their power with the nobility and various forms of popular representation (which cannot be equated with modern parliaments). Monarchy only became absolute in some European states in the early modern period, when monarchs reached for dictatorial power and philosophers such as Hobbes, Machiavelli and Bodin provided the theoretical legitimization for this. This phase lasted until the French Revolution at the end of the 18th century.[8]

In view of the social upheavals associated with this development, such as the abuse of power and oppression, but also the civil wars in England, where the king's expansion of power was successfully, but bloodily, prevented, classical liberalism emerged. On the one hand, its pioneers stood in opposition to the princes' encroaching usurpation of power. On the other hand, they did not adopt the radical programs of the republicans on the other side. They deduced which functions the state had to fulfill for the good of the general public, for what purpose governments were to be used and how the abuse of the power conferred could be counteracted. In doing so, they drew on biblical teachings in many respects and laid the foundation for the Christian approach to politics that I would like to present in this book. Therefore, on the following pages I present a selection of what I consider to be the most important liberal thinkers in order to base all further explanations on them.

3.3.2 – John Locke

The English physician and philosopher John Locke was born on 29.08.1632 and died on 28.10.1704 - the very time when the English people prevented absolute monarchy, established a republic for a time and finally restored the constitutional monarchy that still exists today. With his work "Two Treatises of Government", he laid the foundation for liberal state theory and is therefore also known as the father of liberalism.[9]

In the first of the two treatises, Locke refutes Sir Robert Filmer's treatise on the justification of absolute monarchy, which was widespread at the time but was treated rather secondarily in its later reception. In the second treatise, "On the True Origin, Extent and Purpose of State Government", he elaborates on his understanding of the state. This is the actual foundation of the liberal theory of the state, which is why I will discuss it in detail.

Without the existence of state order, Locke sees man in a state of nature:

"It is a state of complete freedom (...) without asking anyone's permission or being dependent on the will of another. It is also a state of equality in which all power and jurisdiction are reciprocal, since no one possesses more than another"[10]

Later he writes:

"I maintain (...) that all men are by nature in that state and remain in it until they make themselves members of a political society by their own consent."[11]

He goes on to describe the state of nature:

"In the state of nature there is a natural law that binds everyone. (...) For all men are the work of one almighty and infinitely wise Creator, the servants of one sovereign Lord, at whose command and on whose behalf they were sent into the world. They are his property, since they are his work, and he has created them to exist as long as it pleases him, but not as it pleases them among themselves."[12]

Locke thus defines as a basic law of human coexistence that no one has the right to kill a fellow human being on a whim, because God, as the author of life, also has the sole right to decide on its end. However, as the transgression of this law is not excluded in the state of nature, jurisdiction lies in the hands of the individual:

"That all men may be restrained from infringing the rights of others, and from injuring one another, and that the law of nature, which requires the peace and preservation of all mankind, may be observed, the execution of the natural law is in that state placed in every man's hands. Thus everyone is authorized to punish the violators of this law to the extent necessary to prevent a recurrence of the violation."[13]

The fact that everyone thus becomes a judge in his own cause and a war of all against each other threatens, results in the willingness of individuals to unite in political societies that protect their respective rights. Locke writes about this:

"But since no political society can exist without a power within it to protect property and to punish for this purpose the transgressions of all who belong to this society, there is a political society only where each of its members has given up his natural power and renounced it in favor of the community (...). In this way, the personal judgment of the individual members is eliminated, and the community becomes the impartial and sole arbiter for all, according to fixed, standing rules."[14]

According to John Locke, the basic prerequisite for the formation of such a society to protect life and property from encroachment is voluntariness:

"Since men, as has already been said, are by nature all free, equal and independent, no one can be expelled from this condition and subjected to the political power of another without his consent."[15]

For submission to a government, a distinction is made between tacit and explicit consent - the former comes about very quickly:

"Every man who has any property, or enjoys any part of the dominions of a state, gives hereby his tacit consent. (...) and in its ultimate effect it may even consist only in any person's being within the territory of that government."[16]

The difference to explicit consent is described by John Locke as follows:

"If, therefore, the owner (...) gives up the said property, he is at liberty to go and annex himself to any other state, or to agree with others to establish a new one in vacuis locis, in any part of the world which they find free and ownerless. On the other hand, he who has once, by actual consent and express declaration, given his consent to belong to a state, has bound himself for ever and irrevocably to be its subject and to remain so unalterably."[17]

According to Locke, the state's remit is clearly defined, because people submit to it in principle with three objectives: "for the mutual protection of their lives, liberties and property".[18]

In this sense, a political society is first and foremost an institution to protect people from foreign encroachment. Government action cannot therefore be arbitrary and any intervention by the state in the affairs of its citizens, in particular the restriction of freedoms and access to the property of members of the community, is impermissible unless the consent of the persons concerned has been given in one of the above-mentioned forms.

In order to maintain the legitimacy of governance, Locke defines four limits that must not be exceeded:

- "First, it must govern according to publicly promulgated, fixed laws, which may not be changed for special cases"
- "Secondly, these laws shall be directed to no other end than the welfare of the people"

- "Third, they may not levy taxes on the property of the people without the consent of the people themselves or their deputies"
- "Fourth, the legislature shall not and cannot delegate the legislative power to any other, or in any other manner invest it than the people have done"[19]

I recognize in John Locke's thoughts a large part of the principles that can already be derived from the Mosaic Law.

3.3.3 – Charles de Secondat, Baron de Montesquieu

In some respects, I see Charles de Secondat, Baron de Montesquieu (18.01.1689 - 10.02.1755) as the younger French or continental European counterpart to John Locke. The lifetimes of both authors overlapped by only a few years. Nevertheless, a common thread runs through the traditional thoughts of both men: the rejection of the abuse of power. While Locke derived fundamental theses on the functioning of states from his experiences in the English Civil War, Montesquieu was concerned with how these states and their laws were shaped under different geographical and social conditions. He observed:

"The law is, generally speaking, the common sense, in so far as it governs all the nations of the earth. The state and civil laws of every nation must be nothing else than the particular cases to which this common sense is applied. They must be so peculiar to the people to whom they are to apply that only by a great coincidence can they be appropriate to another people."[20]

Montesquieu distinguishes between republican, monarchical and despotic governments, whereby the first form is characterized by the fact that the people or a part of them hold the political power, while the other two forms of government are each characterized by the rule of an individual and differ in the question of whether this rule is bound by fixed laws or not. In the case of republics, a distinction is again made between democracies and aristocracies, depending on whether the whole people or only a part of them share political power.[21]

In the further course of his work, he explains which differences in climatic location, the size of a country and the prevailing religion favor which type of rule in his view.

In general, the republic form of government is suitable for small states, while medium-sized states tend towards monarchy and very large states very easily fall into despotism.[22]

Montesquieu writes about the influence of Christianity: "The Christian religion is far removed from pure despotism, because the meekness so praised in the Gospel is opposed to the despotic fury with which the ruler would take revenge and commit his atrocities. (...) How admirable: the Christian religion seems to have only our happiness in the afterlife in mind and yet helps us to our happiness in this life too."[23]

Within Christendom, the author sees a republican tendency among the Protestant peoples of the north, where he assumes a greater striving for freedom and independence, while he believes that monarchy is better suited to the Catholics of the south, who are loyal to the Pope.[24]

In my view, two remarkable recommendations can be found in Montesquieu's remarks on the relationship between state and religion.

The first demands that religious ideals should not be enforced with the power of the law. The example cited (in a work published in 1748!) is compulsory celibacy: "Celibacy was a recommendation of Christianity. When it was made a law for a certain class of people, new ones were needed every day to persuade people to observe this law. The legislator plagued himself and plagued society in order to implement it by decree. As a recommendation, those striving for perfection would have observed it."[25]

Here he expresses what must be a basic premise of every Christian state: That everyone is responsible for their own salvation and that no worldly power can impose a supposed or actual path to spiritual perfection on its citizens.

The second recommendation relates to the issue of religious tolerance. Montesquieu states: "As soon as the laws of a country have come to terms with the admission of several religions, they must also oblige them to tolerate each other. (...) If the state gets on well with the religion already established, it is therefore an excellent civil law not to permit the introduction of a new religion. (...) If one has it in one's hands whether one wants to give room to a new religion in the state or not, one should not let it in. If it has already been admitted, it should be tolerated."[26]

This view is, at least from today's perspective, somewhat ambivalent and takes some getting used to. However, it fits very well into a consistently liberal understanding of the state. Based on the assumption that a state is a voluntary association of individuals, the common religion can certainly be defined as the unifying element that is a mandatory prerequisite for joining the state. However, if the state system is a compromise between the different groups of a heterogeneous society (and this is the case in modern Western states), a commitment to a religious confession would be an impermissible interference in the structures that have evolved.

Probably Montesquieu's best-known "invention" is the separation of powers. Although he never used this term himself, as far as I know, he formulated its content. The basic idea is as follows:

"So that power cannot be abused, it is necessary to arrange things in such a way that power restrains power."[27]

To this end, he distinguishes between three powers of the state:

- Legislative power is used to pass, amend and revoke laws.
- The executive power ensures the implementation of laws and internal and external security.
- The judicial power ensures that disputes are decided in court.

To prevent abuse of power and loss of liberty, these three powers or authorities must never be delegated to the same persons or bodies. As the holder of legislative power, Montesquieu quite naturally assumes a body made up of several individuals (apart from the divine legislation on Mount Sinai, I cannot think of any non-despotic state in which the legitimate legislative power would have rested with a single individual). This body should not be constantly active so as not to interfere with the execution of the laws once they have been passed. In his eyes, executive power must be entrusted to a monarch in order to enable swift action. The author also emphasizes that it would be contrary to the separation of powers and thus to the safeguarding of liberty if the executive were to be determined by the legislature (because they would effectively be in one hand). To avoid a despotism of the legislature, Montesquieu advises giving the executive a right of veto over the decisions of the legislature and also entrusting it with the power to decide when the legislature should meet. In return, the executive must not have any positive decision-making power in the legislative process. He also recommends a temporary body for the judicial power.[28]

In the general direction of thought, Montesquieu and Locke agree, as already written. However, it is noticeable that Montesquieu (although he was the younger of the two) placed much greater value on established structures and the traditional status quo. On the one hand, this can be seen as a certain conservative bias (although he was certainly not seen as a conservative by his contemporaries), but on the other hand it can also simply stem from his broad view of the different states and peoples of the world. While I see Locke as the theoretical foundation of modern liberalism, I regard Montesquieu as a pragmatist who saw the art of politics in working with what was already there. This is precisely why it is so valuable to see both intellectual greats in a common context.

3.3.4 – Adam Smith

Adam Smith was a Scottish philosopher and economic theorist who became known primarily for his extensive work "An Inquiry into the Nature and Causes of the Wealth of Nations". In this book, he sets out his understanding of a free market. He also explains which geographical and political conditions can influence economic development.

For example, he writes about the advantages of coastal countries:

"Since water transportation opens up a more extensive market for every kind of industry than land transportation alone can provide, it is the sea coast and the banks of navigable rivers where industry of every kind begins to divide and perfect itself; perfection often does not extend to the inner parts of the country until long afterward."[29]

While Adam Smith is generally rather reserved about state intervention in the economic cycle, it is very clear from his statements that he sees monetary policy as a task for the state. For example, he recommends levying a coinage fee for the issue of a gold or silver currency:

"A small minting fee on gold and silver would probably give the minted pieces of these metals an even greater preference over the uncoined ones. Coining in this case would increase the value of the coins by this small fee, just as, for the same reason, the mold increases the value of tableware by the price of the mold. The preference of coins over bars would prevent the melting down of coins and discourage their export: If a state need should make it necessary to export money, most of it would soon return of its own accord. It could only be sold abroad according to its weight in bars; in the country, however, it would be worth more than this weight: therefore it would be a profit to bring it home again."[30]

Smith regards the circulating money of an economy as a tool to keep the exchange economy running. In this sense, he considers it desirable for the currency itself to tie up as little capital as possible[31]. In this sense, he advocates the use of paper money:

"The substitution of paper for gold or silver money replaces a very costly means of payment with a far less costly and sometimes equally suitable one. Circulation is brought about by a new wheel that costs less to produce and maintain than the old one did."[32]

Regarding the origin of money, Smith explains that after people began to divide labor, it became necessary for everyone to build up a stock of their own products and other people's goods that exceeded their own needs in order to be able to exchange the products of other people. As a result, generally recognized means of exchange became established all over the world, mostly in the form of precious metals.[33]

Smith cites inflation as a difficulty that has existed at all times. In its most widespread form, it has always been caused by governments reducing the metal content of their coins over time, thereby diluting the value of the currency.[34]

But he also points out that even the actual value of a particular precious metal is not stable:

"However, gold and silver, like every other commodity, are also changeable in value, sometimes cheaper and sometimes more expensive, sometimes easier and sometimes more difficult to buy."[35]

3.3.5 – Silvio Gesell

Silvio Gesell cannot be considered a liberal in the true sense of the word. In his book " Die Natürliche Wirtschaftsordnung " / "The Natural Economic Order", he combines liberal and socialist points of view in a remarkable way. "The elimination of the unemployed income, the so-called surplus value, also known as interest and rent, is the immediate economic goal of all socialist endeavors"[36], he writes in the introduction to his work and agrees with this goal without advocating direct expropriation[37]. He attests to the fundamental depravity of nations and states: "Nations are always inferior to their constituent parts. Man does not win where he shifts the responsibility for everything he does to the masses: in the community, man acts more shabbily than individually."[38] He deduces that, because God has given the earth to the children of men as a whole, the claims of individual peoples and states to their territories are unjustified and consequently freedom of movement and settlement for all people in all countries should be sought and all national and private land ownership should be abolished, which would automatically lead to the dissolution of nation states.[39]

Logically, these demands should result in a kind of world government that can effectively prevent the emergence of new claims to ownership and state territories. This is precisely where I see the weak point in Gesell's model of society, because no one can guarantee that this world government could not lead to a world dictatorship and that the lesser evil of individual states would be replaced by a much greater one. After all, if nations act "more shabbily" than individuals, as Gesell himself says, how much shabbier must a "world community" act?

However, there are two demands in Gesell's work that every liberal and libertarian should think about, because these are the most justified points of criticism of modern liberalism and capitalism:

1. That the possibility of accumulating property over generations (creating unequal starting conditions for people from birth) should be restricted.
2. That hoarding as a store of value is an abuse of money as a means of payment that should be avoided wherever possible.

I also find both ideas in the Bible (see the division of land in ancient Israel and the resulting tenancy law for 1. and Jesus' reference to the deterioration of earthly treasures through rust and moths for 2.) and I am convinced that they can be easily reconciled with a libertarian social and economic order. I will go into this in more detail in later chapters.

3.3.6 – Milton Friedman

While Gesell cannot be described as a representative of liberalism in the true sense of the word, I would not consider Milton Friedman to be a representative of Christian liberalism because, unlike the aforementioned, he lived and worked at a time when Christianity had already lost enormous importance as a yardstick for political action. I do not wish to pass judgment on his personal life of faith, because only God can fathom that. I have not found any biblical references in Friedman's undoubtedly liberal to libertarian argumentation, but he elaborates on Locke's and Smith's thoughts, so that his work can be helpful to us in various ways:

1. As a continuation of the thoughts of earlier authors in the context of our modern times
2. As a deepening of the liberal principle with regard to economic and social policy (Friedman was first and foremost an economist)
3. As a guideline for political action in predominantly non-Christian existing societies

Friedman formulates his understanding of states in very sober terms in the introduction to his bestseller "Capitalism and Freedom" - in deliberate contrast to authoritarian approaches:

"For the free citizen, however, his country is the assembly of the individuals who make it up, nothing outside or even above him. The free citizen is proud of the common heritage and loyal to common traditions. But he regards the state only as a means, as an instrument, and not as a dispenser of favors and benevolent gifts or as a lord and god whom he must blindly obey and serve."[40]

This sentence is one of the ones that makes my heart beat faster when I read it, because I can completely agree with this refreshingly sober and non-ideological view. A state or polity has its justification - as a means to an end. As Christians, we know that some kind of order is also wanted by God. But it must not take the place of God and become an idol, which would ultimately be the consequence of statism and all collectivism. Friedman continues in this vein, following on from John F. Kennedy's inaugural address:

"The free citizen will neither ask what his country can do for him, nor what he can do for his country. Rather, he will ask: 'What can I accomplish with my countrymen with the help of the government' - in fulfilling my individual duties; in achieving our individual goals and purposes; and above all, in preserving our individual liberty. (...) Freedom is a rare and delicate plant. Our reason tells us, and history confirms it, that the great danger to liberty lies in the concentration of power."[41]

He concludes from this that government power must be limited and should be distributed wherever possible. In this sense, he essentially advocates limiting the activities of the state to the protection of freedom and centralizing political decisions as little as possible. He advocates the principle of strict federalism (no exercise of power should take place at a higher level than absolutely necessary).[42]

I interpret this approach as a transfer of the market economy principle to the socio-political sphere: wherever possible, different approaches to solutions should be able to operate side by side. As the world is divided into different states, each of which pursues different sovereign approaches in fields such as state structure, defense, fiscal or health policy, and some or all states are made up of subordinate units, which in turn have their respective competencies, there is free competition for possible solutions to any issue. If the chosen path of a state or part of a state turns out to be a dead end, successful approaches of other states can be followed. Individual citizens have the opportunity to change their place of residence or even the state, so that the individual political units must always ensure that they create an attractive living space for a sufficient number of citizens.

I can warmly recommend anyone who is or would like to be involved in politics and economics to read Milton Friedman for themselves. He has a very clear writing style and astutely refutes a large number of modern fallacies. I could cite many more quotes, but I don't want this chapter to degenerate into a collection of quotes. I would like to conclude this first insight into Friedman's world of thought by explaining how he understands the term "liberalism" and what misunderstandings have become associated with this term over the course of time:

"When an intellectual movement called 'liberalism' developed in the late 18th and early 19th centuries, it emphasized freedom as the highest goal and saw the individual as the highest being within society. The movement supported laissez-faire as a means of internally reducing the role of the state in economic affairs and strengthening the role of the individual. Externally, it supported free trade as a means of uniting the nations of the world peacefully and democratically. Politically, this movement supported the development of representative democracy and democratic institutions, the restriction of state despotism and the protection of individual civil liberties. In the late 19th century - and especially after 1930 in the United States - the term 'liberalism' was used with a very different emphasis (...) (...) The 19th-century liberal regarded the extension of liberty as the most effective way to achieve the social state and equality. The 20th century liberal saw general welfare and equality as prerequisites or alternatives to freedom."[43]

He vehemently opposes this turn of the concept of liberalism into its opposite. In contrast to this modern so-called liberalism, the term "libertarianism" (adjective: "libertarian") has developed and established itself in recent decades to describe the original and consistent liberalism. Milton Friedman's grandson Patri Friedman, among others, is categorized as a libertarian. Accordingly, in the following chapters

I will also use the term libertarianism throughout, which corresponds to what intellectual greats from John Locke to Milton Friedman understood as liberalism.

3.3.7 – Hans-Adam II. von und zu Liechtenstein

Hans-Adam II von und zu Liechtenstein is de jure the current reigning monarch of the dwarf state of Liechtenstein, although he handed over the reins of office to his son in 2004. In 2003, he enforced a new constitution, which was the first constitution in the world to explicitly stipulate a right of separation for regional authorities (in this case the individual municipalities of the Principality). I have not yet read through his several hundred page work "The State in the Third Millennium". However, Titus Gebel, whom I will introduce in the next section, refers to this and in particular to the Prince's view that the state should see itself as a service provider for its inhabitants.

3.3.8 – Titus Gebel

In my opinion, the most consistent and pragmatic continuation of the liberal or libertarian idea comes from the pen of Dr. Titus Gebel. He has been campaigning for the establishment of independent private cities for several years and in 2018 published the book "Free Private Cities. Making Governments Compete For You", the third edition of which was published in 2023 and to which I will refer below.

He sees the defense of individual freedom as the most important task of a state or state-like system:

"The only real problem with mankind is that people seek to impose their will on others. The task is therefore to create an order which prevents this from happening."[44]

He describes global government activities as the largest market in the world, which is crying out for optimization and more competition:

"The market of living together is not only the most important, but also the largest market. State activitiy accounts for approximately 30% of gross domestic product of all countries. Nonetheless, the performance is poor. (...) Any reasonably skilled entrepreneur should be able to do better. If one could somehow offer the services of the state and at the same time avoid its pitfalls, more and more taxation and paternalism while constantly changing the rules of the game, then a better product will have been created."[45]

The omitted passage in the above quote contains a list of state mismanagement and obvious state failures and crimes.

Titus Gebel uses the history of the Federal Republic of Germany to show how today's democracy is increasingly encroaching on citizens' freedom of choice. A small minority of politicians decide how citizens should behave. On the one hand, they do not have the option of freely agreeing (or not agreeing) to these rules and, on the other hand, they must pay for all the costs caused by politics. Gebel opposes the familiar form of democratic co-determination with the principle of self-determination, which essentially states that any legal obligation to which a person is subject must be based on their voluntary consent.[46]

In principle, this demand corresponds to that of John Locke centuries earlier.

He therefore regards the forced redistribution of modern welfare states as unjust and postulates:

„The welfare state corrupts people by promoting antisocial behavior. (...) The demand of social groups for redistribution, which is omnipresent in the welfare state, is also tantamount to calling for a crime. Because redistribution is only possible by taking away the fruits of others' labor. The consequences are never-ending fights for distribution, social discord and envy."[47]

Gebel concludes from this that more and more interest groups are approaching the state to demand support and enrich themselves with taxpayers' money. These groups shy away from stealing themselves and send the state to rob their fellow citizens. As more and more people take the path of simply getting money with the help of the state, the proportion of productive people decreases over time and at the same time those who remain are increasingly restricted and exploited.[48]

In contrast to the current trend towards the centralization and unification of states, Titus Gebel sees it as an absolute necessity that as many independent states or communities as possible exist. This is because competition is the only way to effectively limit the power of the government and thus prevent the abuse of power.[49]

Dr. Gebel introduces the concept of free private cities as an alternative and competition to conventional state systems:

"Imagine a system in which a private company as a "government service provider" offers you protection of life, liberty and property. This service includes internal and external security, a legal and regulatory framework and independent dispute resolution. You pay a contractually fixed fee for these services per year. The government service provider, as the operator of the community, cannot unilaterally change this "citizens' contract" with you later on. (...) You take care of everything else by yourself, but you can also do whatever you want, limited only by the rights of others and the other moderate rules of living together. (...) Disputes between you and the government service provider are heard in independent arbitration courts, as is customary in international commercial law. If the operator ignores the arbitral awards or abuses his power in another way, his customers leave and he goes bankrupt. He therefore has an economic risk and therefore an incentive to treat his customers well and in accordance with the contract."[50]

According to this concept, free private cities would compete with the existing states and with each other for inhabitants. The mere possibility of emigrating to such a private city could sooner or later create an incentive for governments to be less wasteful with their citizens' assets. More importantly, however, it would provide a real alternative for everyone, and especially for society's top performers, offering legal certainty and freedom.

In my view, the fact that the city operator could in principle become insolvent is very interesting. After all, it is precisely the (not entirely unjustified) belief that states cannot go bankrupt that tempts those in power to constantly embark on new spending orgies. The possibility of insolvency would very probably prevent them from using other people's money to finance their ideological plans. At least if they were personally liable.

Since different people have different ideas about living together, Titus Gebel sees enormous potential for diversification and great flexibility in free private cities, for which he also presents various examples.[51]

The prerequisite for the establishment of free private cities being accepted by existing states (which today control almost the entire usable surface of the earth) is today - just as in the Middle Ages when free imperial cities emerged - the advantages that such a city can offer the state that provides a piece of territory for it. For example, the economic revival of the directly adjacent surroundings can be such an advantage (examples of such an effect are the city-states of Hong Kong, Singapore and Monaco, which have contributed significantly to the development of the adjacent areas of their neighboring states). Where such effects are realistic, there is also a realistic chance of persuading the relevant governments to make small territories available and to relinquish sovereign rights to these areas in whole (which is rather unlikely) or in part (which seems much more likely). Suitable locations for such projects are more likely to be found in less developed regions of the world than in modern industrialized countries.[52]

Titus Gebel takes up the idea of the social contract, which has been in use since the time of Locke and Montesquieu, and develops the principle of an actual contract from this abstract and fictitious agreement, which each citizen concludes with the operator of their private city and which codifies the mutual rights and obligations of citizens and the community. This civic contract is thus an individually ratified constitutional document that can only be amended by mutual consent.[53]

The citizens' contract should specify which services the private city must provide to its citizens, which legal regulations and rules of conduct the citizen is subject to within the city, which termination options both sides have, and which sanctions apply in the event of breaches of contract. For disputes between a citizen and the operator of a city, an arbitration court outside the jurisdiction of the private city is recommended.[54]

With the right of termination, Gebel clearly goes beyond the understanding of John Locke, who saw the explicit consent to a social contract as a lifelong binding decision (see above).

I see in Dr. Titus Gebel's statements not only the most practicable continuation of classical liberalism or modern libertarianism, but also the concept with which believing Christians are most likely to make a positive difference in a post-Christian world. We will not be able to significantly improve existing states on their own. The design of libertarian alternative systems and the resulting competition are more likely to succeed.

I came across Titus Gebel's book when I was already in the process of writing this book. I had already developed many of Gebel's ideas myself in a similar form and put them down on paper before I read his book. One example of this is the observation that the greatest driving force for the positive development of social systems does not lie in the co-determination of the broad masses (even if I do see positive aspects in this co-determination), but in the competition between as many independent alternative systems as possible. Another example is the idea of designing the social contract as an actual contract that is signed by the joining citizen upon admission to a community and that clearly defines their rights and obligations.

For this reason, I see Titus Gebel and the Free Cities movement, which he was instrumental in bringing to life, as natural allies and consider the founding of private cities to be the most promising way to establish a Christian community.

4 – Sovereignty and international tolerance

Fortunately, there is not just one single polity on our planet, but a multitude of competing states. Since all people are fallible and therefore no government and no form of government is beyond all doubt, I believe that a unification of nation states into a global system is only desirable on the condition that the omniscient God himself takes over the personal reigns. I am convinced that this will happen one day. Anticipating this and striving for a unification of individual states under human leadership carries the terrible risk of a tyrannical world dictatorship - the Bible knows this scenario as the reign of the Antichrist.

For this reason alone, I believe it is extremely important for the well-being of humanity as a whole that there are as many different states or polities as possible and that they are as independent of each other as possible in political terms. The usefulness of different states also arises from the fact, already established by Montesquieu, that different regional circumstances require individually coordinated laws.

Apart from the fact that it is already clear from the history of the people of Israel that God intended the Jewish community to be a blessing for the whole world, but nevertheless in its direct sphere of influence on a clearly defined territory, the division of humanity into different communities can also be easily deduced from the ancient philosophers and our liberal and libertarian thinkers.

As has already been explained, the thinkers of antiquity shared the conviction that different good and bad constitutional forms alternate during a state's history. When a polity reaches a state of ochlocracy or tyranny, the citizens have the option of emigrating and, at a certain point, this alone puts pressure on the rulers of the state in question to moderate themselves in order not to lose their own people. The mere possibility of intervention by another state or by opposition figures acting from exile and thus difficult to control also mitigates the consequences of a state that has come apart at the seams. However, if this polity were to encompass and control the whole world, such influences would be absent and an inappropriate and misanthropic form of government could become entrenched in the long term.

In short: competitive pressure, which already has predominantly positive effects in other areas, above all the economy, is also advantageous around states. The more different polities there are on earth (potentially competing for inhabitants), the more opportunities there are to optimize social processes for the general benefit.

When Locke writes that a political society can only be formed through the voluntary association of individuals, the question must be asked as to whether it is even conceivable, given the different cultures and characteristics of people, to establish a state to which every individual can consent. In this case, the explicit consent of all would be necessary, as tacit consent always presupposes the possibility of emigration, otherwise it would be a matter of forced consent. From these considerations alone, any form of human world government must be illegitimate if there is even a single individual who does not consent to it. In this sense, every human being would also have the right to resist such a government unless he or she has expressly consented to it.

However, in a world of different states, the question arises as to how these states should deal with each other. What interests can or should a polity pursue beyond its borders? To what extent can states join and form common institutions? Locke gives us the basic answer to this question when he lists the four limits of legislative power:

- "Second, these laws shall be directed to no other end than the good of the people"
- "Fourth, the legislature shall not and cannot delegate the legislative power to any other, or in any other manner invest it

than the people have done"[55]

These are rough guidelines that give every government a certain amount of leeway. But both points are extremely important. Every government has been set up to work for the good of its people. That is its purpose and its primary responsibility. A government that neglects the welfare of its own people in order to curry favor with the rulers of other states or, out of altruism, uses the resources and powers of the people of the state to support societies or individuals that are not part of its own polity is committing abuse of power and embezzlement. A government that hands over real sovereign tasks to international organizations without the express consent of its citizens is also committing an offence. Of course, it is the task of a state leadership to represent its own population vis-à-vis other political bodies and, insofar as it is within its mandate, to conclude treaties and agreements with other states. However, a state's constitutional documents and social contracts always take precedence over intergovernmental agreements.

Milton Friedman writes on this subject in connection with his comments on the perversion of the term "liberalism" in the last century:

"Jealously guarding freedom, (...) the 19th century liberal favoured political decentralization. Completely absorbed in action and trusting in the benefits that result from state power, (...) the 20th century liberal favors centralized state power. He would dispel his doubts as to where state power should be located by arguing that it was better placed in the state than in the city, better in the federal government than in the state, and ultimately better in a world organization than in a national government"[56]

In the original sense of liberalism, handing over political decisions to international institutions is extremely questionable overall. Intergovernmental institutions such as the UN, the EU or similar are useful insofar as they contribute to the agreement of trade relations, to freedom of travel or to better understanding between states and thus to the simpler settlement of interstate conflicts. However, the moment a government allows other states or international organizations to intervene in the internal affairs of its political society, a border is violated and an injustice is committed.

Conversely, this also leads to the conclusion regarding the sovereignty of other states. If a government justifiably rejects any attempt to intervene in its internal affairs from the outside, it cannot expect other states to tolerate interference in their internal affairs. This principle of mutual non-interference applies universally. It is true that it cannot be assumed that every government in the world is based on a voluntary social contract and certainly not that every state has a liberal or even libertarian social order. In principle, however, it can be assumed in most cases that even dictatorial regimes have the tacit consent of the population (provided there is at least the theoretical possibility of emigration). History shows countless examples where well-intentioned interference ended up causing worse conditions than it was intended to remedy. Even in the case of a totalitarian system that holds its population captive, the risk of doing more harm than good through intervention is very high. For this reason, and because a government is fundamentally only responsible for the welfare of its own people, interference in internal affairs should only be an option in very exceptional cases. Both the interventions of Western states in various parts of the world and, for example, Russia's belligerent encroachment on Ukraine are examples of the fact that even interventions in the sovereignty of other states, which are justified by superficially understandable intentions, cause more harm than they could ever do good.

The "right of peoples to self-determination" has played a very dubious role in recent decades. As understandable as the underlying idea is, the use of this principle has mostly led to incredible injustice and bloodshed. For what is to be regarded as a "people" entitled to this right and where the boundaries are to be drawn is entirely up to the observer. With the same right that brought independence to the peoples of the Danube Monarchy and the Poles at the end of the First World War, the Belarusian and Ukrainian inhabitants of the Polish eastern territories could demand their independence from Poland (which was realized at the end of the Second World War, but only to pass directly into the communist dictatorship of the Soviet Union) and the ethnic German inhabitants of Danzig, Austria and the Memel, Saar and Sudetenland territories could demand incorporation into the German Reich. In the same way that the peoples of the former Yugoslavia were able to assert their right to their own states, the Serbs living in Bosnia and Kosovo could and can insist on their right not to belong to these states. Just as Georgia and Ukraine have become independent from Russia and the Soviet Union respectively, the respective populations of South Ossetia, Abkhazia, Donbass and Crimea are free to break away from the two aforementioned states and, if necessary, join the Russian Federation. However, there are two main challenges here:

1. no "people" is a homogeneous mass that could have a common will.
2. there is only a realistic chance of achieving state independence where there are powerful external allies (which is why all attempts by Catalonia and the Basque Country to gain independence from Spain have so far failed), which in turn exert enormous influence on the "independent" state.

If you look at the examples cited, the independence efforts of recent decades (which are always understandable from an individual perspective) have mostly been paid for with a lot of innocent blood. I dare to question whether this is justifiable.

On the other hand, according to the liberal understanding of the state, membership of a state is always voluntary and coercion is always an injustice. In this respect, it always seems advisable in foreign policy, where the question of a territory's independence from an existing state is concerned, to support this in principle, but to work towards ensuring that both the interests of the resulting smaller state and the parts of the population of the independent territory that may not be interested in separation are taken into account. Measures for this can be very individual. For example, financial compensation for the loss of territory could be agreed. Secured access to existing trade routes and extraterritorial transport routes could also be suitable means of ensuring that separation proceeds peacefully.

5 – Constitution of Nova Nicaea

61

5.1 – Central constitutional principles

From the third chapter, we can summarize some principles that should be fundamental to building a polity. The following remarks represent my idea of the completed final stage of Nova Nicaea's development. Since I believe that, at least for the time being, realization is more feasible in the form of a free private city (or as part of one) according to Titus Gebel's concept, not everything will be fully realizable immediately, but that is not a bad thing.

The first and most important principle must be voluntariness. I have already explained in several places that membership of any state should be voluntary and that a newly established Christian polity in particular must consist of voluntary citizens. God does not force us to do anything, so we should not force anyone else to do anything either.

Furthermore, at this point I repeat the constitutional principles derived from the provisions of the Mosaic Law:

- Responsibility of state leadership towards God
- Federalism
- Selection of public officials according to ability and trustworthiness
- Rule of law and legal certainty
- Monarchy and divine right
- Constitutionalism
- Principle of "first among equals"
- Separation of powers
- Information of the population

These principles should be reflected as far as possible in the constitution of the Christian polity. In practice, this means that ...

- ...as form of government, the monarchy is preferable to the republic (the monarch as "first among equals", as a symbol of divine nobility and accountability to God, and as patron of the principles described here)

- ...responsibilities should be divided as far as possible (this applies both horizontally in the sense of separation between the legislative, executive and judicial branches and between church and polity, and vertically in the sense of federalism)
- ...both the constitutional order itself and the laws based on it should change as rarely as possible
- ...the basic rules of coexistence (i.e., the constitution and the laws) must be kept as compact as possible in order to give citizens the opportunity to know them all and apply them at any time
- ...despite the possible democratic participation of the will of the people in legislation and the development of the polity, mechanisms always exist to ensure that public officials are also professionally qualified and that no majority decision is able to bend applicable law or restrict the civil liberties of individuals

In the following sections, I will outline the details of how I envisage it. Of all the existing territorial states, I see these constitutional principles best implemented in the United Kingdom of Great Britain and Northern Ireland, which is why many parallels become apparent. However, I also see major weaknesses in the United Kingdom at some crucial points (such as the lack of codification of the constitution and the ever-increasing number of laws and the resulting limited legal certainty). Everything I write here about Nova Nicaea's future constitution is my draft. I do not presume to believe that this draft is perfect. Therefore, when it comes to the actual implementation, I am open to discussing suggestions for improvement and alternatives and incorporating them if necessary. Nor do I rule out the possibility of different Christian polities forming in the future, for example in the form of several private cities. In the case of a sufficiently large contiguous territory, I would even expressly advocate the federal coexistence of several Christian polities competing peacefully with each other. A confederation (with the option to leave at any time!) of ideologically very different private cities or microstates that share certain infrastructures and form a free trade zone, for example, is also conceivable.

5.2 – The social contract

In order to establish a polity on a voluntary basis, an agreement is needed between the individuals involved. For this reason, and because citizenship is always associated with rights and duties, these should be regulated in a contract that everyone who wishes to become a citizen of the polity must sign and which should also contain provisions on how the contract can be terminated and membership of the polity can be withdrawn. This combines the principle of voluntariness with a certain degree of commitment, which is essential for living together in a civil society. I would set a fixed period of notice for the citizen to terminate the social contract but allow for the possibility of termination without notice in the event of a constitutional amendment. Termination by the polity should only be possible for serious offenses and violations of the social contract and can certainly be used as the most important sanction in criminal law (analogous to banishment from ancient states). As long as Nova Nicaea is "only" established as a private city and not as a fully sovereign state, a major advantage is that every immigrant retains their previous citizenship and cannot become stateless even if the social contract is terminated. However, if full state sovereignty were to be established one day, the person concerned would be threatened with statelessness. In this case, it should be ensured that Nova Nicaea continues to regard the "dismissed" citizen as its own citizen in an international context (and represents him or her vis-à-vis other states) until he or she has acquired the citizenship of another state.

The basic requirement for accepting citizenship is a profession of Christian faith (as summarized in the Nicaean Creed) and a valid baptism with water in the name of the Father and of the Son and of the Holy Spirit. The profession of faith can simply be printed in the text of the contract and is thus signed by the new citizen. The valid baptism should be substantiated with some kind of document (baptismal certificate, extract from the church register, declaration of baptismal witnesses, etc.), a copy of which should be attached to the contract. In exceptional cases where the validity of the baptism cannot be clarified, the new citizen should alternatively be given the option of conditional baptism (baptismus sub conditione), the certificate of which then serves as proof.

5.3 – Ecumenical community instead of state church

At the point where it must be determined whether a potential citizen has been validly baptized and, if necessary, a conditional baptism is performed, the essential difference between Christian polity and the secular state or even ideologically neutral private cities becomes apparent. Here, there is a need for cooperation between the authorities and church officials. Close cooperation between secular government and church is also necessary or at least desirable on other occasions in a Christian polity: the anointing and coronation of the monarch, prayer and penitential services in the event of social emergencies, state funerals - to name but a few.

As long as the church was undivided, such tasks could have been carried out by the respective local clergy. In European countries, they have always been taken over by clergy from the respective state church in the past. In Great Britain, for example, it was the Church of England.

I highly recommend that any interested reader watch the video recordings of the coronations of King Charles III and Queen Elizabeth II (the anointing was not recorded because it was not considered appropriate for the sacredness of the act). These services beautifully express the position and responsibility of a Christian monarch towards God on the one hand and towards his people on the other. In my opinion, the Christian polity of Nova Nicaea should by no means do without such a dignified and meaningful inauguration of the head of state. Not only the fact that God's blessing is prayed for in a very special way on this occasion speaks in favor of such a ceremony, but also the fact that the monarch as well as the other officials and all citizens are reminded in a very impressive way to stand up for the Christian principles of their polity.

For a Christian polity that takes the separation of church and state seriously and wishes to remain neutral towards the different faiths of Christianity, the establishment of a state church is out of the question. Nevertheless, to provide the state authorities with a point of contact in religious matters, I propose the establishment of the aforementioned ecumenical community, which would be located in Nova Nicaea's center. I have the Communauté de Taizé in mind as a model for such a cross-denominational fraternity. Since a Christian polity should have a central church building for urban planning reasons alone, the ecumenical community could be located directly at this church building and be given responsibility for its administration. The clergy of this community should not be bound by any external ecclesiastical institution (such as the Pope or an Orthodox patriarch) but should nevertheless have an ordination that is recognized by as many parts of global Christianity as possible. In my view, the most effective way of ensuring this is for the ecumenical community to be led by a bishop in apostolic succession who does not belong to either the Roman Catholic or the Greek/Russian Orthodox Church. This bishop can bear the title "Bishop of Nova Nicaea", hold services in the city church and appoint clergy to the community, who in turn are deployed wherever the state is dependent on ecclesiastical support. At the invitation of other parishes, these clergymen can also provide administrative assistance there, but neither the bishop nor other clergymen in the community have the right to interfere in the affairs of other parishes. So much for my naïve idea of how one could ensure the necessary ecclesiastical support of the polity without founding a state church.

Such a community can take on further useful tasks for social life beyond the points mentioned so far. Since the members will live in a kind of modern monastic community (I personally advocate that they should not have to be celibate but can have families who are then also part of the community), they can take on social tasks, especially in the early stages of polity-building. Temporarily, they can support the care of the sick and elderly and contribute to the reclamation of the land, as monks and nuns did centuries ago. They may be able to maintain a first school and establish a theological university.

If the city church is designed in the style of a cathedral, it can have several small side chapels that can be made available to small, still developing congregations for their services until they can afford to build their own place of worship. Finally, the ecumenical community can be a point of contact for such emerging congregations and Christian communities that need support in organizational matters (for example, in finding a suitable building site for a church). In the event that a congregation in Nova Nicaea disbands or dies out, the ecumenical community can take over the fiduciary administration of the church building and return it to a worship purpose by transferring it to another congregation for use that does not yet have a building.

5.4 – Duties of citizens

In addition to valid baptism and acceptance of the creed, citizens must agree to the current version of the Nova Nicaea constitution and undertake to obey the laws in force in Nova Nicaea. In addition, anyone wishing to acquire the rights of a citizen must contribute to the building and maintenance of the state. This contribution should consist of two elements:

- a one-off contribution for admission, which can either be paid in a fixed sum of money or through charitable work on the Nicaean infrastructure.
- a permanent obligation to pay a monthly or annual fee, which may be reduced or waived in return for the assumption of security, national defense or civil defense tasks

I will discuss the second point in more detail in the chapter on defense, military and civil defense. The Nova Nicaea government can determine the extent of the contribution to the intake as required and use it as a means of controlling the influx.

If a welfare system is set up (I will also discuss this in a later chapter), a kind of deposit should be charged when people move into the polity, regardless of the fee for becoming a citizen. This should be calculated in such a way that it would cover possible financial benefits from the polity over a period of, for example, 5 years. If the funds have not been used during this period, the deposit can then be paid out or offset against any fees due. This prevents deliberate immigration into any existing social systems (more on this in the chapter on economic and social policy).

5.5 – The Nicaean monarchy

The Mosaic Law already clearly prescribed constitutional monarchy (even if this was not realized until centuries later), the ancient thinkers considered mixed forms of government to be desirable and Locke and Montesquieu also clearly tended towards moderate monarchy. In the Christian states of the past, we find monarchy very frequently and the most stable state system of the former Christian peoples to this day, namely the British, is a constitutional monarchy. Because scripture and tradition clearly coincide here, Nova Nicaea should also have a monarch at the head - at least if the degree of sovereignty achieved in each case allows this.

A monarch is an anchor of stability and continuity in the constitution and also offers a beautiful outward sign that all power in heaven and on earth emanates from God, who is the King of kings, through the divine office and the associated anointing and coronation by the Church.

In principle, there are two forms of monarchy: the elective monarchy and the hereditary monarchy. In biblical times and also in most Christian states, hereditary monarchy was a tradition - and it stands for the principle of continuity in a very special way. Elective monarchy, on the other hand, is typical of ecclesiastical dignitaries (the Pope, for example, is in principle nothing other than an elective monarch of the Roman Catholic Church) and is also very stable in this area. In political systems, on the other hand, elective monarchy was rather rare and, where it was common, rather unstable (e.g., Polish aristocratic republic, Holy Roman Empire of the German Nation). While elective monarchy has proved its worth in the ecclesiastical sphere, hereditary monarchy is therefore more advisable in the bourgeois polity.

While the succession to the throne in the Kingdom of Israel was apparently regulated arbitrarily (the succession of the eldest son was not mandatory, as can be seen from Solomon), primogeniture (i.e., the priority of the firstborn) was generally prescribed in the later Christian royal houses and the succession to the throne was therefore biological. This clearly regulated succession has great advantages: on the one hand, it rules out disputes over the succession to the throne from the outset, and on the other, it ensures a legitimate successor even in the event of catastrophic accidents, such as the extinction of an entire royal family. If a nuclear bomb were to explode in London today, killing the entire immediate royal family, it would still be possible to identify a clear successor to the throne, as the British line of succession includes several hundred distantly related individuals scattered around the globe. In a sense, it is in God's hands which person is placed at the head of a monarchy and when. This aspect, which particularly emphasizes the spiritual significance of God's grace, should be considered when drafting the Nicaean constitution.

However, a fixed succession to the throne also entails the risk that a completely unsuitable person will have to be enthroned. European history has known many a mentally ill prince, so this danger should not be underestimated. I therefore propose a fixed line of succession that is laid down in a law of succession to the throne. In order to preserve the peculiarity of hereditary monarchy, this law should not be subject to the usual legislative process, but should only be passed and amended by a specially constituted body.

In addition to selected representatives of the legislature and representatives of the ruling house chosen by the monarch, members of this body should also include the Bishop of Nova Nicaea (who may personally anoint and crown the next monarch) and other clergy to support him. While I would like to keep the ecclesiastical structures out of all other parts of the building of the polity, at this point it is very important to me that ecclesiastical dignitaries are involved. This is due to the special spiritual nature of the office of monarch. Here we are dealing with the hinge between polity and church. While every other government office, regardless of its practical importance, is ultimately a purely profane office and therefore, for example, a chancellor or prime minister is not usually inaugurated in a church ceremony, a duke, king or emperor is ultimately a placeholder for the one true King, Jesus Christ. Just as a bishop, pastor or church leader, when he leads the service of a church congregation, to a certain extent represents our Lord and Savior in his activity, so does the monarch in the polity. Therefore, the monarchy is also a symbolic subordination of the polity to the heavenly regiment of God and the monarch is thus both a constitutional office holder and a spiritual person. Incidentally, the King or Queen of Great Britain and Northern Ireland is also regarded as such by the Anglican Church.

To summarize: Nova Nicaea was to be structured as a hereditary monarchy, with succession to the throne based on a fixed law that was passed and could be amended by a specially appointed body, the Throne Council. Since monarchs already bore the title of king in ancient Israel and this title was also widespread in Christian monarchies and still is today, it is logical that the monarch in office in Nova Nicaea is also a king. However, this is not mandatory.

But what does the king do once he has been appointed by the law of succession and anointed and crowned by the Bishop of Nova Nicaea? As in all European monarchies, he naturally takes on many representative tasks, from the official appointment of various government offices to speeches to the people on various occasions, to diplomatic visits and receptions. However, the most important task of the king is to maintain the Christian-libertarian polity's character. He stands for continuity and legal certainty and must see his first duty as protecting the population from unlawful encroachments by the government. Two things must therefore be absolutely guaranteed:

1. The king must have no legislative power of his own and no governmental responsibility or jurisdiction.

2. On the other hand, he must be able to intervene in the political process and consistently prevent undesirable developments.

Therefore, the king's most noble right is an absolute right of veto over all government and parliamentary decisions. If he makes use of this right, he must of course justify his decision. We can see in almost every country in the world that governments tend to extend their powers further and further and to regulate all areas of life. This tendency can quickly lead to a loss of civil liberties, so in case of doubt it is better for a royal veto to leave an existing loophole in the law than for citizens' freedom to be lost bit by bit.

The king should also have other powers related to the right of veto:

- the dismissal of the government or individual members thereof
- order early elections to the chambers of parliament (but not dissolution without timely replacement)
- order the retrial of a court case (at the request of one of the disputing parties)
- Pardoning convicted criminals (however, there must be a very clear legal framework for this to prevent arbitrariness)

Equipped with these powers, the king (or queen) of Nova Nicaea is far more powerful than most of today's European monarchs and a real safeguard against abuse of power in government, parliaments and courts. On the other hand, the Nicaean monarchy is a far cry from the absolute monarchy of past centuries. Thus, there is a guarantor of freedom, legal certainty and continuity of the constitution. The constitutional monarchy is the anchor of stability and the protective shield of the Nicaean constitution.

As long as there is no full state sovereignty and it seems inappropriate to appoint a formal head of state, consideration can be given to temporarily placing the duties of the monarch in the hands of the head of the ecumenical community (in my conception, the bishop).

5.6 – Implementation of the balance of powers

The principle of the balance of powers is essential, i.e., the principle that no one individual may wield so much power that it is likely to be abused. In the previous section, I showed that the monarch, who himself has no authority to make political decisions, has the right of veto as a corrective to all other constitutional bodies and, if necessary, can also arrange for the replacement of parliamentary chambers and government offices. Normally, however, it should not be necessary to intervene in this way. It is therefore crucial that the three powers of the judiciary, executive and legislature are consistently separated and decoupled from each other.

In particular, this also means that no one is allowed to hold several public offices, especially not offices from the different powers. This is a point that is not properly observed in many European countries. Members of government are often also members of parliament. This creates a conflict of objectives, as parliaments have the task of monitoring the government and approving or rejecting its plans (if they affect the legal situation or the state budget). An executive that controls itself by overlapping with the legislature and approves its own proposals contradicts the principle of the balance of powers. This is why a government should never be elected by the chambers of parliament that are responsible for its control. Such a procedure always leads to coalition governments that rely on a parliamentary majority, whose members of parliament, conversely, have at least a perceived obligation to support "their" government. To illustrate the undemocratic consequences this can have, I would like to give a very simplified example:

Let us assume that a parliamentary election campaign in an exemplary country at an exemplary time is dominated by the following three exemplary issues:

- Legalization of certain drugs
- Introduction of a statutory minimum wage
- Imposing import duties to protect the domestic industry

Three parties are competing for voters' favor:

- Party A: Libertarian, opposes both the introduction of the minimum wage and the imposition of trade tariffs, but supports drug legalization
- Party B: Conservative, opposes drug legalization and minimum wage, but supports import duties
- Party C: Social liberal, in favour of import duties, minimum wage and drug legalization

In the parliamentary elections, all three parties achieve similar results and each account for around a third of MPs. This means that anyone could form a coalition with anyone. If there were no coalition government, every member of parliament would be free to vote according to their conscience and election promises when making decisions. Parliamentary decisions on all three contentious issues would therefore be based on the votes of the majority of the population:

- The legalization of drugs would be decided by a majority of parties A and C
- The introduction of a minimum wage would be prevented by a majority of parties A and B
- The introduction of import duties would be decided by a majority of parties B and C

In this case, none of the parties would have to explain to their voters why they had not kept their election promises, because they all voted as was to be expected based on the election results.

However, if a coalition government must be formed, the parties are forced to deviate from their programs to some extent. Let's assume that parties B and C have agreed on a joint government after the election. To this end, both parties have signed a coalition agreement containing the following agreements:

- The major joint project is the levying of import duties
- The legalization of drugs is something that the conservative Party B is unable to convey to its voters under any circumstances, which is why Party C accommodates its coalition partner here
- In return, Party B agrees to support the introduction of a minimum wage desired by Party C

Due to the need to form coalitions, the parties in this example each give up part of their program - with the result that in two out of three substantive issues, a parliamentary majority votes against most of the electorate. This is a serious democratic deficit which, in my opinion, is given far too little consideration in modern states.

In earlier constitutional monarchies, parliaments were elected by the people and the government was appointed by the monarch. On the one hand, this meant that the monarch had too much direct influence on the government, but on the other hand it often led to a bitter front between the government and the parliamentary majority. Neither is useful for the stability of a state in the long term. In republics where the head of state is also the head of government or appoints the head of government, the head of state is often directly elected by the people. This is the case in France and the United States, for example. In Germany, we have a similar procedure at municipal level for the election of mayors and district councillors. I think this is much more advantageous than appointment by a monarch or election by a parliament. The difficulty here, however, is that in the position in the state apparatus, which tends to require the most professional expertise, the process of personal election places particular emphasis on personal sympathies and antipathies. Here I see a point where the principle from the Mosaic Law should apply, namely that important positions should be filled by proven individuals. I therefore propose a somewhat more technocratic procedure for appointing the head of government and other members of the government, which I will explain below. The key point here is that the government of Nova Nicaea is not intertwined with the parliament.

Since ancient times, parliaments have had two tasks:

1. Lawmaking
2. Control over state finances

According to Locke, the main reason for establishing a polity is to protect individual rights and in particular the right to private property:

"The great object which men entering into a society have in view is the peaceful and safe enjoyment of their property, and the great instrument of this is the laws which have been enacted in that society."[57]

The polity is therefore obliged to be careful with the resources of its citizens. Unfortunately, this principle has been completely neglected in Western countries in recent years (which I attribute in part to the fact that the parliamentary majority and the government are often intertwined). In earlier times, however, a great deal of attention was paid to this. It is probably also due to this that control over tax law and the state budget was referred to as the "royal right" of parliaments. In times when laws were not changed and new laws not created on a monthly basis, the budget debate was also much more central to parliamentary work than is the case today. In this respect, it is also very understandable that the traditional European constitutions did not provide for equal elections for the parliaments, but for different types of census elections. This was an attempt to ensure that those sections of the population who raised the majority of state revenues were also granted the majority of the power to dispose of these funds. In retrospect, this seems strange, but it had an enormous advantage for budgetary discipline: it prevented the majority of those who contributed little or nothing to the financing of the polity from imposing ever new burdens on the minority of high achievers and, with the help of the state, making a prey of the income and assets of their fellow citizens.

Universal and equal voting rights are a relatively late phenomenon in most countries. It is based on the idea that, in principle, every citizen is affected by legislation and therefore every citizen should have an equal say in the legislative process. As equal voting rights have become established since the end of the 19th century, there has unfortunately also been an explosion in public spending and the burden of taxes and duties, which is still increasing today, slowing down economic development and thus also the further development of living conditions.

Both approaches have their pros and cons. That's why I would simply combine them and divide the parliamentary tasks. While decisions on the state budget and legislation regarding taxes and duties are taken by a parliamentary chamber elected on a weighted basis according to tax revenue, all other decisions can be discussed and decided in a parliamentary chamber elected by universal and equal vote. However, since the decisions of this second chamber can also have an impact on state finances and the economic functioning of society, the first chamber should be granted a right of appeal against these decisions. I refer to these two chambers below as the Upper Chamber and the Lower Chamber.

If Nova Nicaea is founded as a private city and is run by a company with the intention of making a profit (e.g., a public limited company or a cooperative), the upper chamber can also be replaced by the assembly of shareholders. Since their individual profit prospects depend on the financial decisions of the community, the shareholders have the greatest possible interest in ensuring that the finances are handled economically and sparingly.

It could be argued that two chambers cause more effort and therefore higher costs than a single-chamber parliament. I believe the advantage that the combination brings justifies this expense. After all, the upper chamber prevents the country from slipping into an ochlocracy, while the lower chamber prevents the emergence of an oligarchy. Properly set up, a parliament does not have to be very expensive. After all, in a state that values legal certainty and continuity, there is no need to have a permanently sitting parliament:

"But since those laws which are to be constantly executed and whose force is to be permanent can be created in a short time, it is not necessary for the legislature to be always in office, because it is not constantly busy."[58]

The parliamentary chambers can therefore consist of honorary members of parliament who earn their income in the private sector, just like any other citizen. They do not receive a salary, but at most an expense allowance. This makes parliamentary work interesting for people who have already proven themselves elsewhere and who really care about serving society. On the other hand, such an activity is highly unattractive for people who have never pursued a value-adding activity and who, in today's parliamentary systems, see the mandate as an opportunity to make money the easy way.

If both chambers of parliament are made up of honorary members, they can also meet at different times so that separate plenary chambers are not required. The sessions can take place in a conference hall that is also used for many other events. Only the Presidium of each chamber (three people should be enough) should be a permanent institution to prepare meetings and, if necessary, invite MPs to unscheduled meetings. The parliamentary chambers should be kept as small as possible to save costs but should also be large enough to represent all relevant social groups. I have in mind a size of around 100 MPs. To avoid stalemate situations in voting, an odd number is recommended - for example 99 members in the upper house and 101 in the lower house. As long as the state is very small, the upper house can also be significantly smaller, and the lower house can be replaced by a people's assembly.

The Nicaean constitution thus has a monarchical element with the king and a democratic legislature with the parliaments. The election of the upper chamber, which is weighted according to tax revenue, already has a slight aristocratic or meritocratic tendency. I consider this to be extremely important to ensure that not only opinion but also expertise flows into political decisions. In parliamentary work, however, the principle of democratic representation of the population as a whole (lower chamber) or the donors (upper chamber) prevails.

The main area of application of aristocratic-meritocratic principles should be in the executive. The aim here is not to reflect the majority opinion, but to implement what has been laid down in the social contract or decided by majority vote as effectively and efficiently as possible. This requires competent and, if possible, experienced people. In order to select and advise these people, I advocate the establishment of a third chamber of parliament, which is already known from the ancient constitutions. This refers to the Senate (in Athens a similar institution was called the Areopagus) as an assembly of proven personalities who are elected to office for life. The advantage of being elected for life is that the senators can make decisions to the best of their knowledge and belief without being driven by fluctuations in public opinion. Such a decoupling from public opinion is helpful for the selection of suitable executive officials and for advisory activities. At the same time, the lack of the possibility of being voted out of office by the population prevents such an assembly from being given legislative powers. The Senate is therefore purely an advisory body and, when appointing government officials, acts as a distance between parliament and the executive to prevent too close an entanglement. Because it does not fulfill a legislative function in the true sense of the word, it should be significantly smaller than the parliamentary chambers. I suggest a maximum size of 33 members (honorary, of course). The upper chamber is best suited as an electoral body (because aristocratic-meritocratic principles are already involved in its composition), but alternating elections by the upper and lower chambers are also conceivable. It should be ensured that the number of senators is odd at all times. Due to the lifelong term of office and the objective of electing proven individuals to the Senate, it would be unfavorable to fill all seats at the same time. It seems more sensible to me to allow the Senate to grow slowly by electing three senators when the polity is founded and then adding two more every year, with the option of electing a third senator as an exception to ensure an odd number of members if a member of the Senate dies or resigns. Over a period of 16 years, the Senate would thus grow to its full size of 33 senators, who would then only have to be filled.

In the case of a private city operated by a company, the senate may be replaced by the supervisory board, provided that the upper chamber is replaced by the general meeting of shareholders.

The Senate is responsible for the composition of the government. When selecting members of the government, the senators are required to choose professionally suitable people without bias. In order to be able to carefully consider the right person for each position, there should be no fixed legislative periods for the government, unlike for the parliamentary chambers. The Senate can appoint members of the government either for a limited period (for a fixed term of office - this is particularly useful if an office needs to be filled under time pressure) or on a temporary basis. This avoids having to fill the entire government within a short period of time, which can lead to superficial scrutiny when selecting candidates. In principle, any citizen who considers themselves suitable should be able to apply for a new government post. It may also be possible to admit external applicants. To avoid overloading the Senate, it can be stipulated that candidates must submit a certain number of supporting signatures as the population grows.

The highest government office is the chancellor as head of government. Suitable candidates for this office are preferably people who have already gained experience in other executive or legislative positions. The chancellor is assisted by ministers for various areas. The following ministries could be firmly anchored in the constitution:

- Finance (administration of the treasury, supervision of any existing central bank and possible financial authorities)
- Economy and infrastructure (coordination of the necessary investments in infrastructure and any existing company investments)
- Foreign affairs (diplomacy and international relations)
- Internal affairs (police, fire department, civil protection and disaster control, prison system)
- Defense (armed forces, border protection and intelligence services)

These ministries cover the basic functions of a polity and should generally be sufficient. If the Chancellor considers that further ministries are required, he must have them approved by the upper chamber (because they must be provided with financial resources). For all its activities, the government must draw up an annual financial plan, the budget, which must also be approved by the upper chamber.

As the members of the government and the authorities under their authority are responsible for the constant implementation of existing law, their official duties are full-time. The chancellor and his ministers are nothing other than the top managers of a more or less large company. Since the tasks and responsibilities incumbent upon them should, as far as possible, be carried out by highly qualified individuals, these posts must also be paid well enough to attract candidates who would otherwise hold top management positions in other areas. However, under no circumstances should they set their own salaries, as the public sector must not be a self-service store. The final decision on the pay of the chancellor and ministers, like all financial matters of the state, lies with the upper chamber. The Senate can make proposals on salary levels.

Finally, it must be clarified how the term of office of a member of the government is terminated. As I wrote above, it is possible for the Senate to award a government office for a limited term. At the end of the predetermined term of office, it must then decide whether the term of office should be extended or not. Sometimes it may make sense to set a maximum limit on the term of office. This, in turn, is not the responsibility of the Senate, but of the lower chamber. Other ways in which the term of office of the chancellor or a minister can end are resignation, death and dismissal by the king. The latter case should only be possible in the event of obvious breaches of duty, or if one of the three chambers of parliament or a referendum expresses a vote of no confidence in the member of government concerned and calls on the king to dismiss them. However, in order to maintain the separation of the legislative and executive branches, a vote of no confidence by the upper or lower chamber must not automatically lead to dismissal. Rather, if it is not possible to smooth the waters and restore confidence, the king must have the option of either dismissing the member of government or calling a new election of the relevant parliamentary chamber.

It is the responsibility of the Ministry of the Interior to ensure that the population is informed about the legal situation. There should be modern digital options for this (e.g., a citizen app). However, as in all other areas of life, including means of payment, every citizen must be free to dispense with the use of digital aids. It is therefore also necessary to publish all legal texts in book form, but to charge a fee to cover the costs of issuing them to the public. In the interests of legal certainty, the Ministry of the Interior must also ensure that the number of laws in force does not get out of hand. Although legislation is a matter for the legislature, members of the government can introduce legislative initiatives in the parliamentary chambers. The Minister of the Interior is therefore free at any time to request the abolition of superfluous laws, to propose simplifications in the content and wording of laws or to suggest the consolidation of laws on related subjects with the aim of achieving the greatest possible general validity. It may also make sense to set a maximum number of words in the constitution that may not be exceeded in all valid laws. This would effectively prevent an increase in legal regulations, as the legislature would be forced to withdraw older laws at a certain point at the same time as new ones are introduced. This also strengthens equality before the law, as such a requirement prevents exceptions in laws.

If the laws are kept so clear that every citizen can keep track of them, every citizen can in principle also participate in jurisprudence. This should be the requirement for a generally understandable law. That is why the judiciary can consist mainly of lay judges. As long as the number of court cases is manageable, this function can be exercised in an honorary capacity. In addition to the lay judges, there should also be at least one judge in each court case who is familiar with the court's jurisprudence and the conduct of proceedings, who presides over the hearings and is responsible for the proper conduct of the proceedings. Lawyers from different states can be appointed for this office when the polity is founded, and specially trained lawyers can then be available for subsequent appointments. For simple hearings, a chamber of one judge and two lay judges is sufficient. The supreme court should be somewhat larger, at least in the medium to long term, in order to be able to deliberate on difficult cases, such as constitutional complaints (provided they are not heard by an external court of arbitration), with sufficient care. I have in mind a panel of three judges and four lay assessors for this case.

To ensure the independence of the courts, I would select judges and lay judges using a procedure that was used in ancient Athens for the selection of many state offices: the drawing of lots. To this end, all persons who fulfill formal and clearly verifiable requirements for these offices (these requirements must be defined by the Ministry of the Interior) must be able to apply for them. Selection would then be random. This not only prevents the politically motivated reappointment of judges (which can be observed in almost all modern states), but also underlines the principle that God himself is the actual supreme judge and that it is up to him, who alone can control chance, to select suitable judges.

In principle, it should be possible for parties to a dispute to appeal to arbitration tribunals in church or private hands as an alternative to the courts of the polity, whose decisions are recognized as valid, provided that both parties have agreed on the respective arbitration tribunal in advance of the process.

5.7 – Federalism

By federalism I mean the principle that every decision should be taken at the lowest possible level: better by the individual than by the family, better by the family than by the civil community, better by the civil community than by the central state and better by the state than internationally. Anyone who has understood and agrees with the principle of the autonomous individual will also see the sense of federalism. The closer decisions are made to the individual, the better they are tailored to the individual's situation and the less they restrict their freedom. The larger a polity is, the finer the federal structure should be. The minimum level of organization is:

Individual - family - polity - global community

This is why, on the one hand, the polity must not interfere with families, but must also be able to guarantee that the individual does not perish within a family. Accordingly, there must be rules as to how far the family's power of disposal over the individual extends.

Within defined limits, the polity must respect the autonomy of the family (interference in the educational methods of the parents and the values they teach is taboo), and outside these limits it must guarantee the rights of the individual. These boundaries are very easy to draw: physical integrity and the age of majority. Within these limits, parents are responsible for their children and the polity must respect their sovereignty. However, if the physical integrity of children is in danger or if parents attempt to restrict the rights of their children beyond the age of majority, the polity must intervene to protect the individual.

The age of majority has been set very differently at different times and in different countries. I am of the opinion that where the church considers its members to be responsible for themselves, the polity should do the same. As far as I know, all church communities that baptize only in adulthood admit baptized persons from the age of 12 to 14 at the latest. In the church communities that baptize children, the respective ecclesiastical acts to confirm the baptismal promises, i.e. confirmation, take place at this age at the latest. Marriages, for example, are also permitted from this age under Roman Catholic church law. I am therefore in favour of recognizing the individual's personal responsibility and independence from parental decision-making power from the age of 14 at the latest.

In a Christian polity, it makes sense to also consider church congregations as a federal authority - at least for all matters relating to church orders. This applies, for example, to marriage law. Marriage was personally instituted by God and is therefore not a state order, but a church order. Where the necessary ecclesiastical structures were lacking or the state wanted to suppress them or bring them under its control, it usurped the right to conclude (and even dissolve) marriages. A Christian polity must recognize that it does not have this right, but that this is a matter for the church congregations. Of course, the polity can demand that marriages be registered so that the spouses can be treated as such. It can also stipulate framework conditions that must be met for a marriage to be legally concluded (minimum age, no more than one simultaneous marriage per person, ban on marriages between close relatives), but must leave the implementation to the church.

Even beyond purely ecclesiastical matters, it can be expedient to orientate the federal structure towards church communities. For the sake of convenience, larger church congregations will find that parishioners will increasingly settle in the immediate vicinity of their church building. If this is foreseeable, it can be offered to this community that the same people who belong to the church community also form a federated unit and that this unit is assigned some of the public tasks. This approach is particularly suitable for communities whose members are also characterized by a particular way of life. The most striking example that comes to mind in this context is the Amish people. But Adventists, for example, could also have their own local authority (assuming there are sufficient numbers), which could then introduce a Sabbath rest for their businesses in their territory instead of Sunday rest.

The federal division according to church congregations is not mandatory, but only one of many possibilities. In principle, as soon as it is possible for the central authority to transfer powers to a subordinate body, this should be done.

Conversely, the principle of federalism also makes it possible for the Christian-libertarian polity of Nova Nicaea to constitute itself temporarily or permanently as part of a larger project and form a federative unit within this project. In this way, it is not necessary to wait until enough believing Christians have been found who want to build a free private city together, but a small group (for example the members of the ecumenical community already mentioned several times) can join forces with other or non-believing libertarian-minded people and build a private city in which Christian community is an integral part. I even see this as a very decisive intermediate stage towards realization (see corresponding chapter).

6 – Economic and social policies

6.1 – Capitalism as a law of nature

I have taken a large part of this section from my book "Gott & Geld" / "God & Money" (in German published only), so it will be familiar to readers who have read that book.

Any Christian with half a brain will realize that the physical, chemical and biological design of the universe is subject to God-given eternal principles - the laws of nature. It does not have to be written in the Bible that gravity is intended by God or that the water cycle is God's will - everyday observation teaches us this.

It gets more exciting when it comes to social and economic contexts. But why? Doesn't the history of thousands of years teach us that the law of supply and demand is just as eternal as the movement of the planets around the sun and that the connection between laziness and misery is just as fixed as the gravitational pull of the earth? Or that economic booms and crises alternate as surely as ebb and flow, as day and night?

I maintain: In the same way that God has ordered the laws of nature, he has also determined the functioning of the economy from the beginning of the world. And the economic order that God created is what modern science calls capitalism or a free market economy!

Anyone searching the internet for the term "capitalism" will quickly come across the following definition:

"Capitalism is an economic system based on the private ownership of the means of production and their operation for profit. Central characteristics of capitalism include capital accumulation, competitive markets, price systems, private property, property rights recognition, voluntary exchange, and wage labor."[59]

What would happen if you put a group of people on a deserted, uninhabited island? Everyone would start using their own skills and abilities to create useful products or services, which they could then make available to others in exchange for other products and services. In this way, the individual characteristics of each person would be put to the best possible use for the benefit of the community. No one would think of investing their energy in something that others do not need, and certainly no one would exchange their product for something for which they have no use (even if this use only consists of exchanging it with a third party for something else). Production is therefore controlled by the market. Over time, a primitive civilization develops: one person cultivates a field and keeps a draught animal for his plough, another domesticates sheep, goats or cattle in a forest clearing, the next builds a workshop for woodworking, perhaps a fourth erects a water or windmill. In short: private ownership of the means of production is created.

So, we can see that the constituent elements of capitalism occur naturally all over the world. Now one could argue that private property is not absolutely necessary - everything could belong to everyone. This objection makes sense, but it is a fallacy - for a very simple reason: ownership is an obligation, non-ownership is not. If something belongs to me, I will ensure that it is maintained - if something does not belong to me, I will not willfully destroy it, but I am also not responsible for its continued existence. A society without property is therefore also an irresponsible society. Admittedly, this point is less obvious than the market principle. However, it seems as if the heavenly Father was keen to make this clear, as we are reminded of this twice in the Ten Commandments alone.

6.2 – Private property

6.2.1 – Acquisition of private property in general

John Locke already dealt with the question of how an individual can acquire property if God has given the earth to mankind for common ownership. His answer is that, in addition to the common property of mankind (namely the earth and everything that it produces by nature), each individual has exclusive ownership of his person and this right of ownership is also transferred to everything that is produced by that person's work or is taken from the state of nature:

"Although the earth and all lower creatures belong to all men in common, yet every man has a property in his own person. (...) So whatever he takes away from the state which nature has provided and in which she has left it, he has mixed with his labor and added something of his own to it. He has thus made it his own. Since he has removed it from the common state (...), something has been added to it by his labor which excludes the common right of other men."[60]

Nevertheless, not one individual can acquire everything:

"The same law of nature that gives us property in this way also limits this property. (...) As much as a man can use to any advantage of his life before it perishes, he may make his labor his property. What goes beyond that is more than his share and belongs to others. Nothing was created by God to be spoiled or destroyed by men."[61]

At this point, the author draws attention to the fact that almost all goods and products are subject to natural decay, which prevents them from being hoarded.

6.2.2 – Private ownership of land and property

When considering private property, the ownership of land has a very special significance because the earth's surface is a good that is almost impossible to increase but is necessary for the livelihood of all people. Accordingly, the question of distributive justice arises here more than with all other goods - because if one person or group owned the entire surface of the earth, the whole of humanity would become dependent on them. It is therefore essential for the freedom of the individual to avoid excessive concentration of land ownership. John Locke derives this from the Bible:

"it is clear in any case that God, as King David says in Psalm 115:16, has given the earth to the children of men, and that he has given it to men together"[62]

Since, as we saw in the previous section, all goods become the property of a person by the fact that this person takes them from the state of nature and makes them usable through his labor, it stands to reason that this is also the case with the soil. Accordingly, Locke states:

"As much land as a man plows, plants, farms, cultivates and as much as he can utilize of the yield, that much is his property. (...) God and his reason commanded him to subdue the earth, i.e., to cultivate it for the benefit of life and in this way to spend something on it that was his own - his labor."[63]

And further:

"God gave the world to mankind in common. But since he gave it to them for their benefit (...), it cannot be assumed that he intended it to always remain common property and uncultivated. He gave it for the use of the diligent and intelligent (...). (...) Thus we see that the subjugation or cultivation of the earth and the exercise of dominion are closely connected."[64]

It follows from these considerations that ownership of land not only obliges people to use it, but that use itself is the prerequisite for establishing ownership. The consequent conclusion from this is surprising for today's libertarians and was also very disconcerting for me when I first read it. That is why I am quoting Locke here in a somewhat broader context:

"Whoever, before appropriating land, gathered as many wild fruits, killed, caught and tamed as many animals as he was able, and expended as much effort on the wild products of nature in order to somehow deprive them of their natural state by his labor, thereby acquired a property in them. But if they perished in his possession without being properly utilized, (...) he violated the common law of nature and made himself liable to prosecution. He impaired his neighbor's share, for his right to these things went no further than his use of them required or than they could serve him for the convenience of life.

The same standard applied to the ownership of land: whatever someone cultivated and harvested, stored and consumed before it spoiled was his special right. Whatever he fenced in, the cattle he fed and the produce he could consume also belonged to him. But if the grass of his fenced land rotted on the ground and the fruits of his planting rotted without being gathered and preserved, that part of the earth, regardless of its boundaries, was still to be considered ownerless and could be taken possession of by another."[65]

According to Locke, fallow land can therefore simply be taken into possession. Land ownership without cultivation is therefore not possible. In this respect, his approach clearly differs from our usual principle that every piece of land (even fallow land) has a fixed owner (who, in case of doubt, can still charge a lease or rent from a fellow human being if they want to use that piece of land).

If we take this principle to its logical conclusion and consider that states are societies of people and can only receive rights from their members that they themselves hold in the state of nature, we can come to the conclusion that a state cannot lay claim to territory that has not been made usable by its citizens or on its behalf. This idea, which goes beyond Locke's argument, means in consequence that all permanently unused territory is either already no man's land or becomes no man's land after a while. A consistent application of this principle would be contrary to the customary practices of international law, as it would entitle anyone to declare new states on any open space. In this respect, it would not be conducive to world peace to insist on it. In the case of international conflicts, however, the position can certainly be derived from this that, in cases of doubt, the right to a territory should be granted to the state to which the people who manage this territory (wish to) belong.

Silvio Gesell is one person who takes this idea to its logical conclusion. He criticized the division of the earth among the various states with the following words:

"The epitome of all international rights is state sovereignty over the land occupied by the peoples. This is also the source of friction, the bone of contention. With the help of this state sovereignty, it has become possible for the world to be arbitrarily reduced in size for man; - ultimately so reduced that he starves, dies of thirst, freezes to death."[66]

Gesell is of the opinion that this international law per se contradicts the biblical tradition:

"According to this international law, He gave the earth - not to the children of men, as it says in the Bible - but to the nations. And what an abuse the nations are making of (...) sovereign rights! Let's take a look at America! Did Columbus discover that part of the world for the North Americans? Certainly not: he discovered the land for mankind, but at least for his compatriots. And today the Americans refuse to allow these compatriots to land on the pretext that they don't know how to write or have no money in their pockets! (...)

True to their slogan "America for the Americans", the Americans are erecting a customs border around the vast territory that Columbus gave mankind (...), so that Europeans must constantly reckon with the possibility that the earth will one day be smaller for them by the entire American continent, or at least by the United States. (...) For them, the economic loss of a continent has exactly the same effect as if it were swallowed up by the sea.

(...) Like the Americans, every nation that has run here, swept up by some tyrant, says: "our country, our exclusive property"!

(...) Here we must fall back on the cell of all states, on the individual. Here we must proclaim human rights, not international rights. And as point one of all human rights: "He gave the earth to the children of men". (...)

Before Moses, Attila and Garibaldi let their fellow peoples degenerate into too much confinement, they look across the border; and if they discover ground there that is less densely cultivated, they go and strike down those who want to deny them access to the earth, citing the rights of nations and scraps of paper. They oppose the sovereign right of nations with the right of man, and in such a war, mankind shall triumph over all nations and their rights.

(...) There are no international rights, no mass rights, no state sovereign rights in relation to the soil and its treasures. International law may only refer to what has been created by human hands. As soon as we grant rights to peoples that go beyond the rights of individuals, such rights turn into war. All men, every single man, has the same inalienable rights to the soil, to the whole globe, and every restriction of this primal right means violence, means war."[67]

As I mentioned in the chapter on Gesell, he sees the gradual abolition of nation states and an international institution for the allocation of land use rights as a possible solution. My opinion is that he overshoots the mark with this, because there is a danger that the concentration of power will open the door to greater injustice than can be prevented.

Despite all current and historical shortcomings, I am convinced that the existence of individual states or sovereign polities is the most important means of limiting the power of individuals over others until the return of our Lord Jesus Christ. Therefore, Christian-motivated politics should avoid everything that leads to its dissolution. By this I mean the dissolution of the fundamental concept of an individual polity. I expressly welcome the fact that a single (possibly failed) state is dissolving and new polities (ideally several smaller ones) are taking its place!

At the level of a polity, however, Gesell's thoughts on land use can certainly be taken into consideration.

Even if it sounds strange to a libertarian and convinced capitalist, I would like to make it clear at this point that I do not consider an absolute right of ownership of a piece of land by an individual to be lawful. I consider the fact that land, regardless of its use, can be accumulated and inherited by individuals and families even if the heirs show no interest in cultivating the inherited land to be even less lawful. It becomes completely absurd when land lies fallow for years or decades, but prospective buyers have no opportunity to make purchase offers to the owners entered in the land register because the land registry is not allowed to establish contact for data protection reasons. Or when people are deprived of ownership of their honestly acquired property, which they have managed for years, because someone claims that generations earlier something would not have been lawful if there had been a change of ownership. On the other hand, it is quite clear that socialist land reforms that deprive the industrious of the land they farm are blatantly unjust.

6.2.3 – Land ownership in Nova Nicaea

How should the issue of land ownership be dealt with in a Christian-libertarian polity? I am very close to Gesell here. In Germany, there are land register and cadastral offices in which every square meter of land is recorded and assigned to a property and its owner. I suspect that there are similar structures in all developed countries at least, which essentially have no other task than to avoid anarchy in land use and thus protect citizens from encroachment on each other's property. In addition, this documentation serves as the basis for levying various taxes and duties.

There should also be something like this in a Christian-libertarian polity - but as a leasehold agency. Land ownership itself should be in the hands of the polity, which has bought the land from its former owners and leases it to its users. Whether the entity holding the property rights is a sovereign state, the operating company of a Christian private city, a cooperative or a polity as part of a secular private city is irrelevant for the time being. Ultimately, land ownership is the most important basis for the legitimacy and feasibility of urban planning measures and regulations as well as for the development of a functioning infrastructure.

However, ownership of the land does not necessarily also apply to the buildings erected on it. Buildings can very well be privately owned, just like all other objects and facilities located on a property.

The purchaser or constructor of a building is obliged to lease the land on which the building stands or to obtain permission from the leaseholder of the land to use the land for this building. In order to ensure planning security, purchasers of buildings must have the option of fixing the lease terms over longer periods (e.g., 50 years). In the case of undeveloped land, on the other hand, the local authority can limit the lease term from the outset if necessary in order to ensure medium-term use for land that is to be available for other projects in the longer term. The more or less strict time limit is likely to lead to more flexible construction methods that are easier to dismantle and recycle, which should result in a better ability to develop the building fabric and would also have a positive environmental impact.

Such an approach creates almost equal access conditions for all citizens to use land.

6.2.4 – The function of money

What is the actual function of money? We should ask ourselves this question, especially as Christians. For the Bible teaches us that we should never allow ourselves to be controlled by money. Money is therefore a tool or an aid, and the acquisition of money is therefore not an end in itself.

There was no money in ancient times. Depending on their skills, different people made goods, bred livestock, offered simple services and bartered with each other. For example, two people could agree that one would help the other build a dwelling for a day in exchange for a chicken or two so that his family would have something to eat.

The more complex and specialized the creation of value in human society became, the more difficult it became to carry out all the necessary transactions with this type of barter. After all, the horse breeder could not pay for his breakfast in fractions of a horse. Therefore, the need arose for a universal medium of exchange that would be recognized within a more or less large circle as a unit of measurement for the value of goods and services. Some cultures used stones shaped into a specific form, other shells and still others small pieces of gold or silver.

Within a certain radius, people agreed to assign a certain value to the corresponding units, which could be exchanged for goods and services. For example, a horse breeder could sell a horse to a king or general and receive a number of mussel shells in return, which he could then exchange for smoked salmon from a fisherman or eggs from a farmer to feed his family. This solved the problem that the producer of a very valuable product was theoretically faced with the necessity of either cutting up his product (and thus often rendering it unusable) or exchanging it for a number of barter goods that he was unable to consume before a natural loss of value occurred, for example through rot or mold.

It is important to understand that this value was ascribed to money by social convention. The units of measurement did not have this value in themselves, just as today a euro or dollar bill is just a piece of paper. The units of shell and stone money were useless objects in themselves. In principle, so are gold and silver bars. Here and there, human bravado led to jewelry being made from the means of payment, which could be used to show off one's wealth. This gave the means of payment a certain practical value that they did not have in themselves. Neither gold nor silver nor stones or shells can feed or warm a person. The original value of these things was simply that they were practical to transport and could be used as a unit of measurement for the value of other things.

The origin of money is therefore the need for a means of exchange or payment. In other words: a currency in circulation.

Throughout history, two problems with money have arisen from time to time:

Inflation

A widespread misconception is that inflation only occurs with today's paper currencies and that precious metal-backed currencies are impervious to it. This is not true. Inflation already existed in the Roman Empire because the Caesars minted smaller and smaller coins and were thus able to produce much more coinage with the same amount of gold or silver than before. After the discovery of America, silver currencies fell into a severe crisis because the treasures captured by the Maya, Inca and Aztecs brought an incredible oversupply of silver to Europe. The Bible tells us a similar scenario from the time of King Solomon:

"All King Solomon's drinking vessels were of gold, and all the vessels of Lebanon's forest house were pure gold, for silver was considered worthless in Solomon's time." (2 Chronicles 9:20)

I probably don't need to explain any further that the risk of an enormous increase in the money supply is even higher with stone or shell money.

But the practical use and circulation of precious metal money also posed major problems for its intrinsic value, which contributed to the breakthrough of paper money, as Adam Smith reported:

"Before 1609, the large quantity of clipped and worn foreign coins, which Amsterdam's widespread trade brought together from all the countries of Europe, had reduced the value of the money in circulation by about 9 percent compared to that of the good newly minted money. As soon as the latter appeared, it was melted down or taken away, as always happens in such cases. Despite the abundance of money in circulation, merchants were not always able to find enough good money to pay their bills of exchange, and the value of their bills became highly uncertain despite a number of regulations taken to remedy the situation.

In 1609, a bank was set up under the guarantee of the city in order to remedy these shortcomings. This bank accepted both foreign coins and the light and worn national coins at their true intrinsic value in good, fully valid national money and only deducted as much as was necessary to cover the minting costs and other unavoidable administrative expenses. For the value that remained after this small deduction, the bank gave a credit balance or credit in its books. This credit was called bank money, which, since it represented the coin exactly according to its denomination, always had the same, real and greater intrinsic value than the money in circulation."[68]

The annoying consequence of inflation is that the price of a product or service in monetary units is higher today than it was twenty years ago. This makes it necessary to constantly renegotiate prices and wages in order to maintain purchasing power.

Deflation

Deflation is the opposite of inflation and is clearly the greater evil. It can also be described as a shortage of money. This problem occurs when either large quantities of the means of payment are withdrawn from circulation (for example, by someone stashing gold coins in a money store) or when the number of users of a currency grows faster than the units available. Prices for goods and services fall because money becomes increasingly scarce. As a result, there is an ever greater incentive for individuals to hoard the means of payment instead of putting it to good use (which in turn can further exacerbate deflation). After all, why should I buy a machine today if I can get two machines tomorrow for the same number of gold nuggets, or why should I hire a craftsman today if I only have to pay him half the price next year? While inflation is primarily a nuisance, deflation can literally strangle an economy.

As people generally tend to accumulate reserves, currencies whose units are subject to little or no natural decay (e.g., precious metals, cryptocurrencies), i.e., which are suitable for bunkering, tend to prevail on the free market. As the corresponding currency units of such currencies tend not to be easily multiplied (or are deliberately capped, as in the case of Bitcoin, for example), there is an enormous risk of deflation (unless a greedy ruler mints ever smaller coins or relieves an indigenous culture of its silver treasures). The social costs of adequately supplying a growing population with a currency consisting exclusively of silver coins, for example, without running into deflation are enormous. This is why, since the Middle Ages, people have increasingly resorted to paper money, which can be easily reproduced. Deflation scenarios can thus be effectively avoided, while the tendency towards inflation and thus the risk of misuse of money production by the state increases.

6.2.5 – Currency system in Nova Nicaea

So how do we deal sensibly with the question of the type of currency?

Titus Gebel represents the most libertarian point of view imaginable:

"The market can decide which currencies are preferred at which conditions and interest rates. In particular, the interest rate should emerge on the market, because otherwise misallocations occur that lead to the waste of resources, bubbles and subsequent crises. If Panama, Liechtenstein or Monaco can do without a central bank, then a Free Private City should be able to manage.

The currency of the host state, a crypto currency such as Bitcoin or a common regional or reserve currency will probably end up dominating the markets or several currencies will coexist."[69]

At first glance, Milton Friedman also seems to share this view:

"The fact is, the Great Depression - like most periods of high unemployment - was caused more by government mismanagement than by the inherent instability of a free market economy. An institution set up by the government - the Federal Reserve System - had been entrusted with the responsibility for monetary policy. In 1930 and 1931, the Reserve System carried out this mandate so ineptly that a minor recession became a major disaster. (...) What we desperately need for a stable and growing economy is reduced, not increased, government interference."[70]

However, he then goes on to say that he still sees the state as having certain responsibilities in monetary policy:

"The main areas of government policy in terms of economic stability are monetary policy and fiscal policy."[71]

I can well understand both opinions and would also rely on the principle of voluntariness here by offering an official currency but not prescribing its use for private and business purposes. This currency does not necessarily have to be administered by a public body or central bank; instead, I would rely on a private-sector initiative that is set up in conjunction with the development of Nova Nicaea and with which the Nova Nicaea project cooperates: a regional currency in the shrinkage money system with partial silver backing.

Sounds absurd? Only at first glance! I agree with Titus Gebel when he calls for competition between currencies to be allowed - which is why, in my opinion, nothing should be prescribed for private or business use. What the customer uses to pay for his potatoes at the greengrocer's is not a matter for legislation but is subject to free agreement between the greengrocer and the customer. On the other hand, I agree with Milton Friedman when he calls for the public sector to guarantee a certain degree of stability. Just as citizens should have planning security regarding the legal situation, there should also be a system of planning security in the monetary area. Above all, this security system should provide a medium of exchange that is secure against deflation and as robust as possible against inflation.

The risk of inflation comes primarily from the internationally circulating uncovered national currencies, while the risk of deflation comes from the increasingly established cryptocurrencies. In the context of a free private city, an additional risk of deflation may also arise if a single precious metal were to dominate as a means of payment. Relying entirely on externally available means of payment can work, but there is a risk of becoming dependent on external currency systems, which can threaten the existence of a sovereign or semi-sovereign system. In principle, I share the ideals of Bitcoiners and other proponents of cryptocurrencies, whose aim is to provide a digital means of payment that is neither dependent on states nor can be controlled by states. As one of several payment options and, above all, as a store of value, I am absolutely in favor of it. However, particularly due to the enormous risk of deflation in the event of intensive use of

Bitcoin and other cryptocurrencies, I believe it makes sense to have an analog alternative.

In my opinion, the goal should be a means of payment that is decoupled from external influences as far as possible (i.e. has no fixed exchange rates to central bank currencies or cryptocurrencies) and offers as little incentive as possible to hoard, so that it circulates as much as possible. Both currently and historically, there are examples of very successful regional currencies with so-called circulation protection. The idea is to build inflation systemically into the individual means of payment (to prevent deflation) but to keep the currency itself stable. The basic idea is to reduce money to its function as a medium of exchange and to deprive it of its function as a store of value, as Silvio Gesell put it:

"Money that becomes obsolete like a newspaper, rots like potatoes, rusts like iron, evaporates like ether, can only prove itself as a medium of exchange for potatoes, newspapers, iron and ether. For such money is preferred neither by the buyer nor by the seller to the goods. People only give their own goods in exchange for money because they need the money as a medium of exchange, not because they expect an advantage from possessing the money.

We must therefore degrade money as a commodity if we want to improve it as a medium of exchange. (...)

We have only to oblige each other to buy immediately and under all circumstances exactly as much as we ourselves have sold, and, in order to preserve the reciprocity of this obligation, to form money in such a way that the seller of goods is compelled by the properties of money to fulfill the obligations connected with the possession of money and to convert the money back into goods personally, if he himself can use goods, through others to whom he lends the money if he does not need goods for himself."[72]

This effect is achieved by maintaining the value of the individual means of payment (banknote, coin, etc.) on certain key dates (e.g. annual or quarterly changes) only by paying a percentage fee.

In Silvio Gesell's concept, a pure paper money system was to be introduced, consisting of bills on the one hand and small change stamps on the other. The bills were to be valid for one year and maintained in value every week by affixing a change stamp equal to one per thousand of the value. New bills should then be issued annually. The loss in value of 5.2% per year would naturally reduce the amount of money in circulation. To prevent currency deflation, as much new money should be printed as is necessary to maintain price stability.[73]

Similar systems have already been used successfully on a small scale:

- After the Channel Island of Guernsey suffered a sales crisis in 1815 because of the Napoleonic Wars, the practice of financing public investments with specially printed money to stimulate the regional economy was established there for a number of years. As soon as the investment had recouped its costs, the corresponding amount of money was destroyed again. This example is seen as a kind of forerunner of the shrinkage money concept[74]
- In the 1920s, the parallel currency WÄRA spread to interested circles in Germany and led to a regional economic boom in Schwanenkirchen in Lower Bavaria and the surrounding area after a mine owner began paying employees and suppliers partly in this currency[75]
- During the Great Depression at the beginning of the 1930s, the Austrian town of Wörgl introduced an emergency currency in the shrinkage money system and was thus able to boost the local economy while the crisis prevailed all around it[76]

- More recently, there have been various regional money projects with circulation protection. Probably the best known is the Chiemgauer in the region around Lake Chiemsee, whose circulation fees are partly used for charitable purposes[77]

The fact that shrinkage money systems can work has thus been proven many times over. The small framework of a city-state, a private city, or a part of it seems to me to be a sensible area of application for such a concept. My basic idea is that precious metals, cryptocurrencies, shares, government bonds or other means can be used to store value and that everyone has the right to do business in cryptocurrencies or foreign currencies, for example. However, for payment transactions within the Christian-libertarian polity, in particular payments between the polity and its citizens, such a circulating secured currency could be established. A devaluation of the bills on a weekly basis, as proposed by Gesell, is not very practicable in my opinion, but an annual or semi-annual rhythm should be feasible.

In order to increase the acceptance of the shrinkage money and its stability, but also to enable a meaningful calculation of exchange rates (and thus avoid a lock-in to existing paper currencies), I would combine the concept with a silver coinage money.

This can be incorporated wonderfully into a shrinkage money system if you follow Adam Smith's recommendation and levy a coinage fee on silver coins. Of course, the reality of life today no longer corresponds to that of Smith's time. On the one hand, international trade is no longer conducted with gold bars and, on the other, there is an international demand for certain coins. The effect he observed at the time, namely that precious metal coins tend to return to the country where they were minted, is likely to have only a limited impact today. However, the essence remains true: minting gives the coin a utility value that goes beyond its material value as an easy-to-handle means of payment. Ultimately, in today's context, the user of a coin system pays a coin fee to cover the additional cost of maintaining this form of cash compared to a purely digital currency. The same applies to the circulation fee for paper money in the shrinkage money system.

If a currency were now to be linked to the value of sterling silver, so that one currency unit corresponds to 10g of sterling silver, for example, coins could be minted with the values 2, 1 and 0.5 of the respective currency unit, consisting of 18g, 9g and 4.5g of sterling silver respectively, and retain their validity for 5 years. After the 5 years, they could only be exchanged for new coins according to their pure material value. This would create a primitive silver-backed shrinkage money system. These coins in combination with bills, which also have a circulation period of five years and are kept in value annually with a fee in the form of a token of 2% of the bill and the corresponding vouchers as small change, would result in a functional cash currency with circulation protection in the form of a loss in value of around 2% of the individual bills and coins.

To illustrate this, I will give the currency the working name argenteus (= Latin for "silver piece") and briefly describe the possible gradation of units:

Nominal value of Argenteus	Value in Sterling silver	Value in EUR on 02/09/2023
Bills		
25	250g	147.50€
10	100g	59.00€
5	50g	29.50€
1	10g	5.90€
Coins		
2	20g	11.80€
1	10g	5.90€
0,5	5g	2.95€
Vouchers		
0,50	5g	2.95€
0,20	2g	1.18€
0,10	1g	0.59€
0,02	0.2g	0.12€

The scale shown above should be sufficient for most everyday transactions and contains a suitable voucher for each bill at 2% of the value of the respective bill. Setting up a suitable giro system or a corresponding cryptocurrency should not be a technical challenge.

The value of the currency would be roughly equivalent to that of the euro if the European Central Bank were to meet its inflation target of a maximum of 2% per annum (which it does not). However, with the following differences:

- Every saver sees how the value of their money decreases from year to year and can act accordingly by investing savings elsewhere.
- As the devaluation affects the individual bill and the individual coin, but not the exchange rate of the currency

itself, the value of prices and wages agreed in the longer term does not change (which leads to greater planning security for everyone)

Either a clear ratio can be set for the amount of money in coins and bills, or (which I think is more appropriate) the currency issuer undertakes to set aside sufficient reserves so that bills can be exchanged for coins at any time on demand. The coin fee and the fee for maintaining the value of the bills should be able to cover the costs of this stockpiling. Another source of revenue could be to provide an advertising space on each bill and sell this advertising space to businesses that accept payments in the currency. In general, the currency should be designed in such a way that the currency issuer at least covers its costs, but ideally generates a profit that goes to the operators or can be reinvested in the development of the polity.

Such a system can be built up in stages. From an organizational point of view, it makes sense to first issue pure paper money backed by stored silver bars before the money supply is large enough to justify the investment in minting technology.

6.3 – Welfare system and public income

It was not so long ago that I considered a certain degree of welfare state desirable. After all, every Christian has a moral obligation to help those in need to the best of their ability. Accordingly, I considered it appropriate that at least an income necessary for survival should be provided by the state. I considered Milton Friedman's proposal to be the preferred method for this:

"The measure that comes to mind on purely technical grounds is a negative income tax. Currently, under federal income tax law, there is a tax-free allowance of $600 per person (plus a minimum of 10 percent for deductible special expenses). If a person earns a taxable income of $100, that is, an income of $100 over the exemption amount and special deductible expenses, they pay tax on it. According to my proposal, if the income is "minus" 100 dollars, i.e. 100 dollars less than the tax-free allowance plus the deductible special expenses, they would pay negative taxes, i.e. receive an allowance. For example, if the allowance rate were 50 percent, they would receive 50 dollars in our example. If they had no income at all and could not claim any special expenses for reasons of simplicity, they would receive 300 dollars at a constant allowance rate."[78]

Friedman's proposal has the great advantage that the required funds are used very sparingly, and the full payment is really only made to people who have no other income, while it is still worth striving for personal income, as the negative income tax is reduced to a lesser extent than personal income increases. I think this rule makes sense wherever individual income is used (and therefore disclosed) as the basis for taxation and this practice cannot be changed. In the Federal Republic of Germany, for example, I would very much welcome the introduction of a negative income tax with the simultaneous abolition of all existing social benefits as a significant improvement on the status quo.

Regarding the existing welfare systems, the negative income tax has enormous advantages in terms of reducing disincentives on the one hand and reducing bureaucracy on the other (the tax offices would replace all state agencies for social benefits and the inefficient state employment agencies could also be closed down). However, this is a treatment of the symptoms. The negative income tax does not attack the root of the state bureaucracy monster. Bureaucracy begins with the state interfering in all the private affairs of its citizens and collecting and evaluating all available data. No working hour spent in tax offices, tax bureaus and companies calculating the taxable income of individuals or organizations is value-adding. Each of these hours is therefore an economic loss and in their entirety, they represent such a huge loss that they can ruin the competitiveness of an economy. For this reason, I would do without any government recording of income wherever possible and prefer to finance the polity from flat-rate taxes or fees. This of course excludes a negative income tax.

Alternatively, only an "unconditional" basic income would be conceivable. I would not make it completely "unconditional" but would firstly link it to the renunciation of all or certain social participation rights (because under no circumstances should the recipients of the basic income be allowed to increase it at will) and secondly to some public service obligations. Street cleaning or the reclamation and development of previously unused land could be carried out at least in part by the recipients of such a public service, and the maintenance of certain facilities and equipment for public defense and disaster prevention could also be assigned to them. Such activities could also be carried out as compensation for fees due.

In the meantime, however, I no longer see the responsibility for social tasks as lying primarily with the state or the civic polity, but above all with families and church congregations. This is because all social measures also require state control to ensure that they are not abused and (as in the case of income tax) to determine the basis for calculating the necessary tax revenue. Families and church congregations do not need such mechanisms, as they can essentially operate through personal contact, mutual trust and a sense of responsibility. The incentive to free oneself from dependence on family or church congregations' contributions is also likely to be much higher than with benefits that come from a largely anonymous government agency.

I therefore propose a largely privately organized insurance system for Nova Nicaea that is essentially based on personal responsibility. Clearly definable life risks such as the risk of illness or loss of working capacity, as well as liability risks and the risk of losing certain assets, can and should be insured under private responsibility. The same naturally also applies to old-age provision. For cases not covered in this way, family and church solidarity is primarily responsible. This mutual responsibility in the personal environment should also increase the willingness to actually insure against significant insurable risks. In this sense, the possibility of support from the polity in the above-mentioned form in return for community service is only the last link in the chain.

Such a lean and decentralized welfare system also allows for a very lean administration of the polity. Especially in the early days with a modest number of inhabitants, most tasks can be carried out on a voluntary basis, as in ancient cities and small states, where even kings sometimes had a normal job. The financial requirements will be correspondingly low. Nevertheless, sources of income are necessary, as the necessary infrastructure must be built and maintained. I see the following as essential sources of income for the polity:

- The admission fee for new residents
- A monthly basic fee for the provision of infrastructure
- Additional fees for the use of services that go beyond everyday needs

- Lease income for land provided for use
- Rental income for buildings (parts of buildings) provided for use that are owned by the polity

These revenues should at least cover the polity's expenses and ideally generate a profit in order to refinance initial investments and enable the further expansion of infrastructure. It is conceivable that fees and lease payments could be waived in certain cases in return for social tasks. For example, as a Christian polity, I consider it appropriate to provide building plots for church buildings free of charge.

As in all areas, alternative concepts should be allowed to compete in a federal system above a certain size.

7 – Education

Just as in all other areas of life, freedom and personal responsibility should also prevail in education. Parents are primarily responsible for the education and upbringing of their children, not the state. Adults are personally responsible for their own education.

However, social coexistence in Nova Nicaea requires a certain level of basic education, which should be ensured. This primarily includes reading and writing as well as knowledge of the relevant language(s) and a basic understanding of numbers. This knowledge is necessary in order to be able to read the legal rules of living together (legal certainty!) and to be able to meet financial obligations as a citizen. Accordingly, the polity has an interest in providing educational opportunities in this regard. However, this does not necessarily mean that schools, for example, have to be run by the polity, and in no case that there is an obligation for anyone to attend certain educational events themselves or to have their children attend them. It is merely a matter of ensuring that access to education exists in principle.

One possibility for this could be that at least public elementary schools are established or the operation of such schools is agreed with private or church sponsors. If attendance at these schools is to be free of charge for pupils and their parents, funding can be provided by private or church foundations and scholarships or, with the approval of the upper house, from public funds. In the latter case, a system of education vouchers can allow parents to choose between different educational concepts.

Education is a market that could be served in a very special way by libertarian polities. Almost worldwide, large parts of the education sector are dominated by state or state-affiliated monopoly providers. This is where Nova Nicaea can make a significant difference by providing complete freedom. Schools as well as vocational training centers, further education institutions and universities can be set up and operated by private and church-run organizations independently of state constraints. In addition to traditional teaching, alternative concepts such as homeschooling, distance learning and online teaching can be offered and even applied beyond the borders of Nova Nicaea. For example, what is wrong with an online university whose students can be spread all over the world?

Private educational institutions, possibly in consultation with the government of Nova Nicaea or educational institutions from all over the world, can define certain educational standards that are taught in different learning concepts but tested in comparable examinations and are thus potentially available to everyone worldwide. In general, I think it is quite likely that libertarian polities and free private cities can become focal points of education and knowledge and thus beacons of civilization in the future.

A current practical example: the Orthodox Church in Constantinople faces a major challenge in ensuring the existence of successor candidates for its patriarch, as the patriarch requires a theological education on the one hand and must be a Turkish citizen on the other due to legal requirements. As the Turkish state has closed all Christian theological academies, prospective theologians have to study abroad and are then regularly expatriated. A distance learning university with a theological faculty could solve this problem.

8 – Language policy

In the previous chapter, I mentioned that basic knowledge of the relevant language(s) is necessary for living together in Nova Nicaea. But which language(s) should actually be spoken in a Christian-libertarian polity? And which languages are used for external communication?

We can and must be pragmatic here. English is currently the standard language in international communication. It is by no means certain that this will remain the case in the long term. At the moment, however, it is a fact. In most future free private cities, which Nova Nicaea could develop into, at least in the initial phase, English will be the predominant language. For this reason, and because knowledge of English is likely to be more widespread among Christians than any other language at present, English must also be the language of Nova Nicaea, at least for the next few years.

However, I see three significant disadvantages in the use of English:

1. the exclusive or predominant use of English harbors the great danger of coming under the strong influence of the English-speaking public and media landscape and of cultivating international relations mainly in the Anglo-Saxon world.
2. learning basic English is easy, but it takes a lot of practice and a good deal of linguistic talent to speak English at a level close to that of native speakers. It can be assumed that immigrants from English-speaking countries will be linguistically superior to all others for a long time within Nova Nicaea.
3. it is essential to study the origins of the Christian church in order to understand the different branches of Christianity. To understand early Christian sources (including the Bible), at least a basic knowledge of the ancient languages is helpful. Relying only on English translations (which are always

influenced to a certain extent by the denominational background of the translators) runs the risk of being one-sided.

In order to counter the first disadvantage, it is desirable that every immigrant maintains contact with the public in their native language and that the information gained from this flows into the common Nicaean public sphere. However, the second disadvantage (the linguistic superiority of native English speakers) tends to be amplified if the media information of all others is provided in their respective native languages. The use of a neutral auxiliary language could counteract this. Before the dominance of English came to full fruition in the aftermath of the First World War, there were some serious attempts to develop a neutral artificial language for international exchange that was as easy to learn as possible. The best-known example is Esperanto - a planned language that has managed to maintain a certain following to this day. Such a language would have the following advantages:

- There would be no native speakers, so that joint communication would take place more at eye level
- Vocabulary, grammar and pronunciation would be so simple that learning them would take significantly less time than learning a natural foreign language
- As an artificial language, an auxiliary language would have less of a tendency to displace native languages

In order to counteract the third disadvantage of the English language, it would make sense to declare one of the ancient languages - Ancient Greek, Latin or even Hebrew - to be the lingua franca of Nova Nicaea.

In this context, I would like to refer once again to the modern state of Israel, which in some respects can serve as a blueprint for Christian polity. Israel today has two dominant languages: English and Modern Hebrew (Ivrit). The use of English came about quite practically during the phase of strong Jewish immigration to the Holy Land. After all, Great Britain was the protecting power of the protectorate territory of Palestine before the state of Israel was founded. Modern Hebrew, on the other hand, is just as much a planned language as Esperanto, for example, but uses the old Hebrew script and has borrowed a large part of its vocabulary from ancient Hebrew. The original Hebrew, on the other hand, has been a purely sacred language for centuries and is only used in Jewish religious services, but no longer as an everyday language. In principle, Hebrew, which was a dead language, has been modernized and revived.

Why shouldn't this also be a model for Nova Nicaea? I have in mind a planned language whose vocabulary is based on ancient Latin and/or Greek and whose grammar is radically simplified compared to the ancient languages. Such a language would be:

- neutral
- easy to learn
- a bridge to early Christian writings and other ancient sources

There are good reasons for using both Ancient Greek and Latin as the basis for this planned language. Both are present in many modern languages through loan words. The main argument in favor of ancient Greek is its use in the originals of the New Testament. The existence of Modern Greek as a living language variant and the comparatively little use of the Greek alphabet in modern times speak against it. Latin's widespread use of the alphabet and its centuries-long use as a language of science speak in its favor. In addition, Latin has an even greater overlap in vocabulary with English and many other languages, especially European languages, than Greek. Many Latin (but also some Greek) words have become internationalisms. One argument against Latin is that it was used almost exclusively in Western Christendom.

My proposal about language policy is to declare English, Latin and Ancient Greek as official languages of Nova Nicaea. In the medium term, a language variant with a greatly simplified grammar could be developed for one of these languages (my personal tendency is currently slightly towards Latin) along the lines of Esperanto and established as a second lingua franca alongside English. As with Hebrew, there would then be an archaic and a modern language variant. Speakers of the modern variant would largely understand the archaic variant due to the common vocabulary but would probably not be able to speak it fluently due to the more difficult grammar. However, old texts could be quoted in literature without any problems, which has great advantages in terms of cultural continuity. An interesting piece of background information: one challenge in the development of planned languages was that there were no old language variants that could be used as stylistic devices. For Esperanto, a variant with linguistic peculiarities was therefore specially developed, which is used in literature as a fictitious old language. I therefore see the parallel existence of an old and a new language variant as a cultural advantage.

The development of the planned language could possibly be carried out by a working group within the ecumenical community, as in a theological context the study of ancient languages is probably still the most lively at the moment. I would be happy to get involved, as I worked quite intensively with planned languages years ago and am currently familiarizing myself with Latin and Ancient Greek. Over time, more and more public communication could take place via this planned language, but probably without eliminating English from use. In the longer term, a situation like that in Israel would develop, with a revived and modernized ancient language as the main language and English as a backup.

I see a particular advantage in the use of a neutral planned language in the fact that (because it is nobody's mother tongue) it has less of a tendency to displace minority languages. There is therefore the option that different language groups (with the corresponding links to the respective countries and cultures of origin) can coexist in Nova Nicaea and form their own federated subjects at a later stage of development. Such a development would certainly be conducive to diversity and internationality.

There will also be various forms of external communication. Depending on the extent to which it is possible to achieve its own state (partial) sovereignty, a certain degree of diplomatic relations will be necessary and desirable. As a neutral polity, Nova Nicaea could one day play a mediating role in the settlement of international conflicts. In the context of such international relations, the use of a neutral planned language (e.g. Esperanto) can be proposed from our side.

9 – Defense, military and civil protection

One of the essential tasks of a polity is to establish and maintain internal and external security. This is probably the justification for the existence of today's world of states. The further the Nova Nicaea project progresses, the more important the issues of defense, military and civil protection will become.

If there is only a low degree of sovereignty, the focus will be on civil protection (i.e. fire department, rescue service and disaster prevention) and internal security (police or security service and protection). However, if (almost) full sovereignty were to be achieved in the further course, the question of a separate military would also arise.

Here I would rely on a mixture of public and private sector players.

The tasks organized by the polity itself can be ensured with a militia system based on the Swiss model. To this end, I propose the establishment of a citizen militia, whose members can be deployed for civil protection tasks as well as for internal security or military defense tasks (if this falls within Nova Nicaea's area of responsibility). Depending on the size of the polity, individual key functions can also be filled full-time. Membership in this militia can either be voluntary and rewarded by a reduction in the annual or monthly fee for Nicaean citizenship, or it can be an obligation under the Citizen's Contract, which can be waived by paying an increased fee. Both options essentially amount to the same thing. The difference is only a question of perspective. I do not consider a rigid obligation without the possibility of exemption to be compatible with the basic libertarian idea; on the other hand, I also do not consider it sensible to completely remove citizens from their responsibility for the security of the polity.

However, there may also be areas that should be handled by specialized full-time staff. To a lesser extent, full-time positions also make sense within a militia system, but not in general. For example, a rescue service should be made up entirely of real professionals rather than militiamen. In the military sector, too, some functions, such as special task forces or a missile defence shield, should be performed by specialized units. In such cases, it makes sense to use private sector providers who can also make their services available to other polities if necessary. For a free private city, for example, it should not be necessary to maintain a permanent military task force. However, as there may be situations that require the deployment of such a force (e.g. if citizens of the private city are taken hostage), it would seem appropriate for such a unit to be set up by a security company and to be able to be called upon by different polities as required. In the more everyday example of rescue services, actors such as the Order of Malta and the Order of St. John have proven their worth.

These or similar organizations could also be commissioned within Nova Nicaea. It may even make sense to transfer certain military tasks, such as border protection, to private military service providers or a modern form of knightly order.

All military facilities in the possession of the Nicaean polity must have a clearly defensive character in order to be able to credibly demonstrate neutrality to the outside world. Military interventions originating from Nova Nicaea must be ruled out. Should individual citizens feel the need to support military activities abroad, they are free to collect money and use it to finance state or private military actors outside Nova Nicaea or to personally join such military endeavors. A libertarian polity must tolerate this as long as it does not compromise the security of other citizens. For the polity itself, however, neutrality is unconditional.

10 – Realization of a Christian-libertarian polity

Having set out in the previous chapters how I believe a Christian polity could be shaped, I would now like to show a way in which such a polity can be established. As I wrote at the beginning of this book, I am convinced that it is possible and desirable to build a Christian polity and that the only thing that matters is to win over a sufficient number of Christians to this idea. I therefore ask every reader who can imagine participating to contact me and pass on or recommend this book to others.

Since an infinite amount of injustice has already occurred in this world (and unfortunately also in the name of the Christian faith), the overriding principle of this project should be not to interfere with other people's rights and customs. Accordingly, I do not see it as an option to "transform" an existing state into a Christian state, as happened in ancient times with the Roman Empire and some other states.

In the following sections, anyone familiar with Theodor Herzl's book "The Jewish State" will notice some parallels. This is intentional - because "The Jewish State" has already passed the feasibility test since the state of Israel was founded. Accordingly, all we have to do is transfer Herzl's concept to the Christian context and our present day and take into account the experiences (good and bad) and mistakes from Israel's history.

10.1 – Sovereignty over a territory

Basically, three things are necessary for the existence of a classic state: a people, a state authority (i.e., some form of government) and a territory. In principle, Nova Nicaea also needs these three things. Any Christian who so chooses can belong to the people of the state. A Government can be established quite easily in the form of a constitution based on a social contract. The big question is that of territory. This question was also the crucial point for Theodor Herzl:

"The whole plan is infinitely simple in its basic form and must be if it is to be understood by all people.

Give us the sovereignty of a piece of the earth's surface sufficient for our just needs, and we will take care of everything else ourselves."[79]

Herzl was thinking specifically of an area in the region of Palestine - and that is exactly what happened. For a Christian polity, it does not matter where it is founded. Two hundred years ago, it would have been easy to find a suitable uninhabited territory that was not claimed by any state (even in Europe, there was still a territory that did not belong to any state until the beginning of the last century: the Svalbard archipelago). Today, things look very different, because apart from a few areas of Antarctica, every piece of land is claimed by some state or other.

In principle, I agree with Locke's deduction that ownership of land can only arise through its cultivation and use and that all unused land is therefore ownerless. If we were to take this further, all unused land would also be stateless, because no community can claim rights that have not been transferred by its citizens. Silvio Gesell takes a similar view. As correct as this derivation is in my eyes, I see a great danger to world peace in its radical application. It is true that we would not objectively harm anyone if we were to set up an infrastructure and declare a state in a deserted territory that is claimed by an existing state but is not actually used. However, such an action would most likely attract at least the mistrust, if not the enmity, of our future neighbors. That would be very unwise.

I would therefore prefer an approach that makes it attractive for an existing state to make such an unused area available to us and to transfer sovereignty over it to us in whole or in part. The benefits we can offer could be of different nature and they are particularly suitable for states that have been disadvantaged in the global economy so far. The simplest incentive could be a sufficiently large sum of money for which we buy or lease a piece of territory from an existing state. If the land is currently unused, the state and its population are not disadvantaged by the sale and the proceeds can be used for public investment as the government in question sees fit. However, there can be even more interesting advantages for a state that arise from the fact that a territory is made available to us for the development of our community. One example is the increased utilization of existing infrastructure (e.g., ports and airports) and the resulting long-term increase in revenue. The creation of jobs in the Christian polity and its surroundings can also bring great benefits to the neighboring country. And finally, there is the opportunity to build efficient infrastructure facilities that also benefit the citizens of the neighboring country (e.g., modern hospitals or production facilities).

It can therefore be assumed that, provided there is a financially strong institution, a state can be found that will cede an unused territory for an appropriate fee and enable the establishment of a new polity.

In principle, such a treaty is conceivable with any country in the world. However, it is particularly attractive for countries with a large area, small population and below-average economic performance. On the one hand, a purchase price can have a much more visible effect on such states than on a large industrialized nation, and on the other hand, the positive effects of mutual economic and trade relations will have a much greater impact on such states.

The most important preparations for the construction of Nova Nicaea are therefore the founding of an organization for the purpose of construction, the search for potentially suitable areas and the establishment of contacts with the relevant governments. In the following, I will simply refer to this organization as the Nova Nicaea Association.

In the following section, I will outline what I consider to be an expedient way of exploiting mutual synergies through cooperation with the Free Cities Foundation, which is already active. I see the advantages of this approach as being, on the one hand, the faster achievement of visible and tangible interim results and, on the other, the opportunity to prove from the outset that our project does not revolve around itself but, despite the independence we are striving for, interacts with the outside world and, in the sense of the principle of "light of the world", radiates beneficially to the outside world.

10.2 – Gradual design

As expected, this book will not become a bestseller overnight. Accordingly, the number of supporters of the Nova Nicaea project is also expected to develop over a longer period of time. Consequently, both a sufficiently large population and a sufficiently large budget to acquire a territory and build a basic infrastructure will not be available immediately. Therefore, I prefer an approach over several intermediate stages:

1. **Foundation of a Nova Nicaea Association and an Ecumenical community.** From the outset, there should be an organizational separation between the spiritual and the political-organizational functions, even if personnel overlaps will be unavoidable at the beginning. A basic ecclesiastical structure is essential for the Christian character of the project and should therefore exist from the outset. However, this structure should under no circumstances be misappropriated for profane purposes, which is why a separate association seems sensible for these purposes. Both institutions can be founded anywhere in the world and be based as soon as there is a sufficient number of founding members (5-7 should be enough). In case of doubt, my private address is available as a working base for both organizations. The tasks of both organizations are networking and promotion in the church sector (Tasks of the Ecumenical Community) as well as networking and representation within the framework of the Free Cities Foundation, acquisition of the necessary financial resources for the next steps and making contact with the key contacts in business and politics (the Association's field of activity).

2. **Relocation of the headquarters of the Nova Nicaea**

Association and the Ecumenical Community to a free private city. On the one hand, as an expression of support for the idea of free private cities in general, and on the other hand, to gain more freedom of action than a place of work within a highly regulated state system allows, the community and the association should settle in an existing free private city as soon as possible. This will also familiarize the main players (including myself and my family) with the day-to-day practice of living in free private cities and gain valuable experience for the further stages of the project.

3. **Establishment of Christian polities as part of free private cities**. Before acquiring an own territory, a sufficiently large number of supporters should already experience life in free private cities. To this end, individual projects can be set up in the private city that houses the Nova Nicaea Association and the community headquarters, as well as in other free cities. These can be individual Christian congregations that settle in private cities and are loosely connected to the community and the Nova Nicaea Association, or well-structured organizations that, for example, set up humanitarian facilities within the free cities in a modern form of monasticism. The establishment of hospitals, schools, nursing homes and other structures can contribute to the overall success of free private cities. Such projects can help to ensure that reducing the state to the bare minimum, as envisaged in the concept of free cities, does not necessarily lead to social coldness, but that social tasks can be fulfilled much more effectively by non-state actors, such as church organizations. It is important here that Christian polities do not attempt to influence the legal system of private cities in their own interests (as Christian churches have unfortunately repeatedly done in the past) and, on the other hand, do not tolerate outside interference in their own affairs.

4. **Building the first Christian free private city.** As soon as the network of interested parties and the population of the Christian polities within free private cities is sufficiently large, the next step can be to tackle a Christian private city of one's own. By then, there will probably already be some experience with the development of private towns and companies that specialize in creating the necessary infrastructure. It may even make sense to have the private city built and developed by an experienced private city operator in the first instance and to buy it from them when the population is large enough to fill all the important functions themselves. In this context, it would be unwise to attempt to transfer the entire population of the Christian communities previously established within secular private cities to the new private city. For a certain proportion of residents, this will be attractive on its own. The others will be happy to remain in their familiar surroundings and, together with the private Christian city, form a network of Christian-libertarian contact points around the globe. Such a network can be incredibly helpful, especially for humanitarian aid campaigns of global significance (for example, in helping persecuted Christians).

5. **Expansion into a Christian-libertarian state.** If the private city reaches its capacity limit, there is the option of building one or more further cities elsewhere (as branch cities, so to speak), which either adopt the tried and tested legal model of the first city or try out modifications of it. On the other hand, there is the option of expanding the private city into a small territorial state by acquiring territory, which in turn can be a confederation of several private cities. Both variants have their charm and at this stage it is too early to decide whether one or the other or a combination of both will be the more sensible option.

The exciting thing about this five-level model is that from level three at the latest, you can easily stop temporarily or even permanently without having gone down the path in vain. If, for example, it does not seem sensible to go to the effort of setting up your own private city due to an insufficient number of interested parties, or if no suitable territory is found for a longer period, you can simply remain as a kind of self-organized part of a private city and work in this area. This means that the final design and speed can remain flexible for the time being.

Five stages in the development of Nova Nicaea

1. **Foundation of a Nova Nicaea Association and an Ecumenical community**	<ul><li>Worldwide advertising for supporters from the Christian spectrum</li><li>Networking in the area of free private cities</li></ul>
1. **Relocation to a free private city**	<ul><li>Expanding one's own scope of action</li><li>Gaining experience in the practice of free private cities</li></ul>
1. **Establishment of Christian polities as part of free private cities**	<ul><li>Broadening the personnel base</li><li>Further experience gained</li><li>Contribution to the success of the concept of free private cities</li></ul>
1. **Building the first Christian free private city**	<ul><li>Own legislation</li><li>Model polity for a Christian society</li></ul>
1. **Expansion into a Christian-libertarian state**	<ul><li>Full sovereignty</li><li>Possibility of confederative</li></ul>

coexistence of different
social designs

10.3 – Colonization of an empty territory

Once a suitable territory has been acquired, colonization must first be set in motion. If possible, the first wave of immigration should include people from different generations. It will have to follow a clear plan in order to avoid important parts of the infrastructure not being available in time. As far as possible, private sector companies should be involved from the outset. The first residential area could be organized along the lines of a club hotel. Such hotel complexes, which can be found all over the world, contain the essential infrastructure that a settlement needs on a manageable scale. Experienced planners for such facilities should be available. In addition to the typical facilities (hotel rooms, suites, pools, restaurant areas, sports facilities), furnished apartments for longer-term use, senior living areas, offices and at least one chapel should also be integrated into the site.

Such a facility can be the first reception point for immigrants and can later be used as a hotel complex and senior residence. Infrastructure facilities can be tested on a small scale before being rolled out on a large scale throughout the city. Ideally, the project should be organized from the outset as a private company (e.g., as a public limited company or cooperative). Alternatively, a public limited company can initially be completely in the hands of the Nova Nicaea Association and gradually be privatized.

To ensure economic stability from the outset, it should be particularly attractive for people who work for clients or employers in their home countries or worldwide, as well as for senior citizens who draw their pensions from their home countries, to settle here. This regularly brings money into the state from outside and boosts demand in the new city to be built and in the neighboring country.

In addition to the residential complex, three other construction projects were to be started at the very beginning:

- a health center with a hospital and doctors' surgeries (should be operational in its basic functions before the first senior citizens move in)
- the basic structure of a representative-technical city center with the central facilities for state construction and a central cathedral including cemetery grounds (the basic structure should be designed to group the city structure around it, but the buildings can be erected gradually)
- this could be followed by a monastery site for the ecumenical community, which would take care of the construction and management of the cathedral and the cemetery and could run a school and a theological university (here too, successive development is possible and sensible)

The planning of the building projects can be carried out by architects and civil engineers who wish to relocate themselves, but it should be done in collaboration with planners from the geographical area in order to take into account the special conditions of the region. I would entrust the construction of the first buildings entirely to local companies. On the one hand, this saves costs compared to companies from industrialized countries and also buys in regionally relevant know-how. In addition, the living spaces will already be ready when the first residents move in.

Annex

A1 – Draft social contract Nova Nicaea

This hereby agrees

.... (hereinafter referred to as "Citizen"),

born on ... in ...

and baptized in the name of God the Father and of the Son and of the Holy Ghost on ... in ...

with the community of all other present and future citizens of Nova Nicaea the following contract:

1. The citizen professes the common traditional Christian faith as it was summarized in the first ecumenical council of Nicaea in Asia Minor in 325 AD. This confession of faith is attached to this contract in ancient Greek, Latin and English and signed by the citizen.

2. The citizen respects the fact that, beyond this confession, there is no complete agreement within Christendom regarding the doctrine of faith. It is respected that there is no complete agreement on either the scope or the interpretation of the scriptures. This fact can be regretted and worked towards rectifying it through understanding. However, no one has the right to impose his interpretation on other Christians. The citizen therefore recognizes as fellow Christians all other citizens who are also baptized in the name of God the Father and of the Son and of the Holy Spirit and who profess the faith laid down in the Confession of Nicaea.

3. The citizen declares his will to live together peacefully with his fellow Christians in Nova Nicaea, respecting mutual rights of freedom, and to respect the written codified constitution of Nova Nicaea attached to this contract and the laws based on it.

4. A one-time entrance fee of the equivalent of YXZg 925 silver

is due for admission to the Nicaean polity, payable either in physical silver or in the currencies and means of payment currently accepted by the Nova Nicaean administration.

5. The contract comes into force upon payment of the entrance fee.

6. A monthly fee equivalent to YXZg 925 silver is due for the provision of the basic Nicaean infrastructure, which can be paid either monthly or annually in advance. Payment is also made either in physical silver or an alternative means of payment accepted by the Nova Nicaea administration at the time.

7. The first two years are considered a probation period. Both the citizen and the administration of Nova Nicaea have the right to terminate this contract at any time at the end of the following month without giving reasons. In this case, the canceled citizen is entitled to a refund of monthly fees paid in advance for future months as well as the full admission fee in the first year and half the admission fee in the second year. The terminated citizen must leave the territory of Nova Nicaea upon payment of the refunded fees.

8. After the two-year probation period, the administration of Nova Nicaea only has the right to terminate the contract in the event of serious offenses against the constitution and laws (regulation according to valid law) or in the event of payment arrears of more than 12 monthly fees. The notice period is two months to the end of the month.

9. After the probation period, the citizen has the right to terminate the contract with six months' notice to the end of the month.

10. At the end of the respective notice period, every former citizen is obliged to leave the territory of Nova Nicaea. There is no entitlement to repayment of fees already paid after the end of

the probation period.

11. Citizens are obliged to participate in the Nicaean Citizens'
     Militia in accordance with the applicable law. Exemption may
     be granted upon request by paying double the monthly fee.

____

citizen Administration of N.Nicaea

A2 – Nova Nicaea constitutional scheme

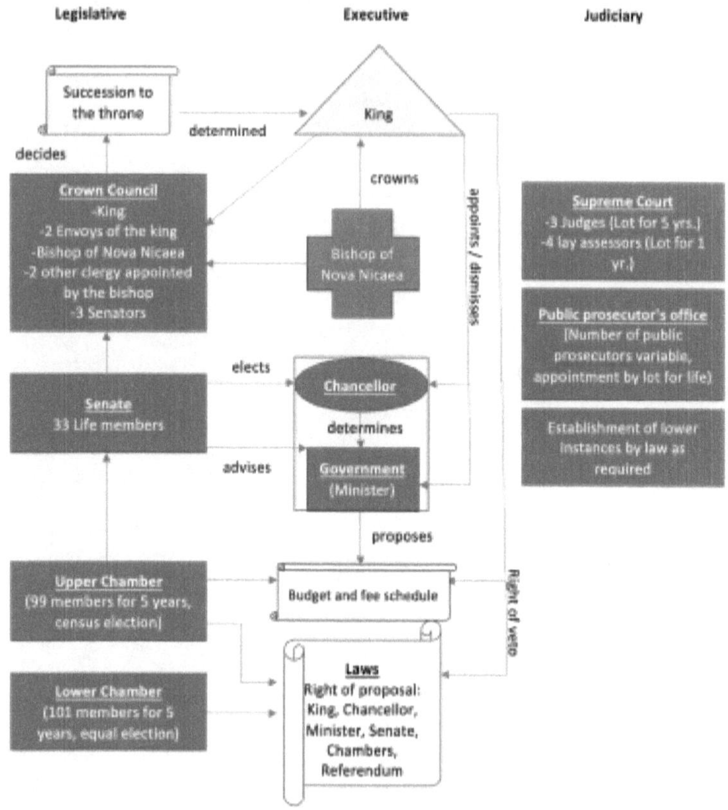

[1] Herzl, Theodor: Der Judenstaat, Jüdischer Verlag, Berlin, 8th edition 1920, p.7 (quoted from German)

[2] Platon: Politeia. 8th Volume, retrieved from https://www.projekt-gutenberg.org/platon/platowr3/staat08.html 12th March 2022 (quoted from German)

[3] Cf. ibid.

[4] Cf. https://de.wikipedia.org/wiki/Verfassungskreislauf, retrieved 12th March 2022

[5] Cf. Vgl. https://www.griechenland.de/athen/, retrieved 19th March 2022

[6] Cf. https://www.bpb.de/shop/zeitschriften/izpb/248544/grundzuege-der-athenischen-demokratie/, retrieved 19th March 2022

[7] Cf. https://www.geschichte-abitur.de/lexikon/lexikon-antike/verfassung-der-roemischen-republik, retrieved 12th March 2022

[8] Cf. https://de.wikipedia.org/wiki/Absolutismus, retrieved 26th March 2022

[9] Cf. https://de.m.Wikipedia.org/Wiki/John_Locke, retrieved 26th March 2022

[10] Locke, John: II. Über den wahren Ursprung, die Reichweite und den Zweck der Staatlichen Regierung, §4 (quoted from German)

[11] Locke, J., §15 (quoted from German)

[12] Locke, J., §6 (quoted from German)

[13] Locke, J., §7 (quoted from German)

[14] Locke, J., §87 (quoted from German)

[15] Locke, J., §95 (quoted from German)

[16] Locke, J., §119 (quoted from German)

[17] Locke, J., §121 (quoted from German)

[18] Locke, J., §123 (quoted from German)

[19] Locke, J., §142

[20] Montesquieu, Charles-Louis (de Secondat, Baron dela Brède et de): Vom Geist der Gesetze, RECLAMS UNIVERSAL-BIBLIOTHEK 1965, 1994, p.104 (quoted from German)

[21] Cf. Montesquieu, C., p.106

[22] Cf. Montesquieu, C., p.197 ff.

[23] Montesquieu, C., p.367 (quoted from German)

[24] Cf. Montesquieu, C., p.369f.

[25] Montesquieu, C., p.371 (quoted from German)

[26] Montesquieu, C., p.387f. (quoted from German)

[27] Montesquieu, C., p.215 (quoted from German)

[28] Cf. Montesquieu, C., p.216 ff.

[29] Smith, Adam: An Inquiry into the Nature and Causes of the Wealth of Nations (German edition: Wohlstand der Nationen. Nach der Übersetzung von Max Stirner herausgegeben von Heinrich Schmidt, Anaconda Verlag, München 2021, p.25 (quoted from German)

[30] Smith, A., p.50f. (quoted from German)

[31] Cf. Smith, A., S.288f.

[32] Smith, A., p.289 (quoted from German)

[33] Cf. Smith, A., p.29

[34] Cf. Smith, A., p.33

[35] Smith, A., p.37 (quoted from German)

[36] Gesell, Silvio: Die Natürliche Wirtschaftsordnung. Neuauflage durch Florian Seiffert Köln 2003, p.9 (quoted from German)

[37] Cf. Gesell, S., p.9

[38] Gesell, S., p.52 (quoted from German)

[39] Cf.. Gesell, S., p.53ff.

[40] Friedman, M.: Capitalism and Freedom (German edition: Kapitalismus und Freiheit). Frankfurt/M., Berlin, Wien 1984, p.19 (quoted from German)

[41] Friedman, M., p.19f. (quoted from German)

[42] Cf. Friedman, M. S.20ff.

[43] Friedman, M., S.23f. (quoted from German)

[44] Gebel, T. : Free Private Cities. Making Governments Compete For You. 3rd updated and expanded edition, Published by Free Cities Foundation, Liechtenstein 2023, p.9

[45] Gebel, T., p.10

[46] Cf. Gebel, T., p.13ff.

[47] Gebel, T., p.33

[48] Cf. Gebel, T., p.34f.

[49] Cf. Gebel, T., p 57f.

[50] Gebel, T., p.98f.

[51] Gebel, T., p.148ff.

[52] Gebel, T., p.172f.

[53] Gebel, T., p.199

[54] Gebel, T., p.201

[55] Locke, J., §142 (quoted from German)

[56] Friedman, M., S.24f. (quoted from German)

[57] Locke, J., §134 (quoted from German)

[58] Locke, J., §143 (quoted from German)

[59] https://en.wikipedia.org/wiki/Capitalism, retrieved 07.11.2023

[60] Locke, J., §27 (quoted from German)

[61] Locke, J., §31 (quoted from German)

[62] Locke, J., §25 (quoted from German)

[63] Locke, J., §33 (quoted from German)

[64] Locke, J., §§34-35 (quoted from German)

[65] Locke, J., §§37-38 (quoted from German)

[66] Gesell, S., p.52 (quoted from German)

[67] Gesell, S., p.53f. (quoted from German)

[68] Smith, A., p.477f. (quoted from German)

[69] Gebel, T., p.273

[70] Friedman, M., p.62f. (quoted from German)

[71] Friedman, M., p.63 (quoted from German)

[72] Gesell, S., p.182 (quoted from German)

[73] Cf. Gesell, S., p.183f.

[74] Cf. https://de.wikipedia.org/wiki/Umlaufgesichertes_Geld, abgerufen am 02.09.2023

[75] Cf. https://de.wikipedia.org/wiki/W%C3%A4ra, abgerufen am 02.09.2023

[76] Cf. https://de.wikipedia.org/wiki/W%C3%B6rgler_Schwundgeld, abgerufen am 02.09.2023

[77] Cf. https://www.chiemgauer.info/, abgerufen am 02.09.2023

[78] Friedman, M., p.245f. (quoted from German)

[79] Herzl, T., p.38